Diary From the Desert

Best Wishes and Reading!! Happy Love, Mary E.

Diary From the Desert

By

Mary E. Stabe

JoNa Books
Bedford, Indiana

ISBN: 1932673105

LCCN: 2003113137

First printing November 2003

To those whose letters fell silent in 1996.
To My Mom, Connie McFarland
To Grandma Dorothy McFarland
To Grandma Pat Stong
To Grandpa Fremont Stong
Wish you were here to see this!

Diary from the Desert

There is an old rickety chair that sits on my Grandpa's porch. It is so old the paint has all worn away and the cane seat has disintegrated and the legs are splintered from where the generations of kittens have sharpened their baby claws. My Grandpa is gone now, but the chair remains. He called me, Mary E.

I come from a tiny speck of a town called Fredericksburg, Iowa. A town where the population swells on the crisp fall Friday nights for the local high school football game. It is a town that despite having the only parade of the year on a Wednesday in June can somehow pull that off with great success and flourish. It is the kind of town I had to leave to learn to appreciate.

We have lived in this neck of the woods for eons and although we've never been rich, we do have the richest, most fertile farmland in the world. Combine that with my family and you have a place where corn and kids grow more than knee high by the 4th of July.

My Dad has been blessed with five children, four girls looking up to one big brother. I am number three. I grew up on our family farm in a traditional "tom-boy" fashion. I loved showing cattle at the State Fair and was a proud member of the Future Farmers of America. I spent more time helping the men folk fix fences than I did in the kitchen, much to my grandmother's disapproval.

My dad once wrote in a Christmas letter that I was at the stage where I was too big to be little and too little to be big. I seemed to have been stuck at that stage for much longer than my mom had hoped. She used to say, "Thank God you weren't a twin!" Dad would say, "Mary has always had a knack for finding herself in the middle of things. There isn't much that hasn't happened to her." Now, I'm not sure if that is good or bad, but I have had quite a few "adventures" in my life.

I graduated from high school in May of 1985 and in the following fall started as a bright faced freshman at the University of Iowa. Unfortunately, that was right in the midst of 80's farm crisis. Money was very tight and, at times, I worked three part time jobs to pay for tuition while taking a full load of classes. At 18, I just wasn't ready to saddle that kind of responsibility, not to mention all those insufferable hours indoor. If only my classes would have been held outside, my schooling would not have suffered so severely. I was drifting through majors and my advisors would admonish me saying, "You are not applying yourself."

Finally, after two years of lackluster performance, I took a break from school. I found myself in Colorado working at a ski lodge. I had a great time, but it didn't do a thing to temper my restless spirit or ground my wandering head.

After the snow melted in Colorado, I went back to our farm to work for the summer. One pivotal afternoon, I came back from the farm early. I had plans for the night. It was one of those early days of summer that was just hot enough to hint of things to come. With me being fresh from the dry, cool mountains of Colorado, the humidity dropped off of me like heavy dollops of rain. I let the screen door slam behind me. I stopped in mid stride, back tracked to the door and bent to take my work boots off.

My mom was sitting on the couch, facing me. The bells and alarms in my head instantly went off and warned me of a serious moment about to arise. Yes, I realized I probably did have mud on my boots, but wasn't I taking them off now? She began with a quiet mother tone, "Mary." There was a long pause while I starred back at her with the most innocent look on my face I could muster. She sighed heavily and continued, "You can't be a ski bum all of your life."

This was not the conversation I expected. The only incisive reply I could muster was "Oh?" I dropped my heavy boot on the floor with a resounding thud. Apparently, this had been stewing on her brain for some time.

My mom was always quick to encourage and support her children, but she rarely ever expressed assessments on our lives. When she made this rare pronouncement, I was jolted out of my lackadaisical stupor. I fully understood what was left hanging between the lines and instantly was overwhelmed by the realization of how badly I was floundering.

Dad, on the other hand, had never found it difficult to make proposals for life adjustments. He and my brother had suggested perhaps I would find some of the "grounding" I so obviously required in the United States Army. I had been in both Air Force Reserve Officer Training Corps and Army ROTC while at the U of Iowa. These courses were some of the minority that I had actually done well. Truth be told the Army just seemed way too ridged and yes, responsible to me.

Yet, after my mom had made her unprecedented proclamation, I consented to at least talk to a recruiter. My father and brother quickly seized the opportunity and loaded me into the pick up. Dad drove and Ken sat on the other side. While I sat between them, I felt as though they believed I would bolt out of the moving truck the closer we came to Waterloo and the recruiter.

I behaved and I was recruited. I signed up for the delayed entry program giving me nearly a year to wait before I actually entered the Army. During the delay, I made another unsuccessful attempt at school and had more fun in Colorado. About a month before I left for basic training my best friend, Dan, and I drove to the park near the farm. We stretched across the hood of my old '66 Valiant looking for falling stars. We weren't talking, just savoring the night when out of the blue I hear, "Mary? Are you really going to go?" I didn't have to ask where. Several of my friends had tried to talk me out of going, but as empty-headed as I seemed to have been during this period of my life, I always kept a promise.

I really had no qualms about joining the military. I sensed I would serve someday or someway. Our family has a great many veterans swinging from the branches of our family tree, starting from the Revolutionary War. Yet, there is always the fear of the unknown and this was definitely uncharted territory for me. I would be the first woman in my family to serve my country and protect the very freedom I had been so reckless with thus far.

So, on June 12, 1989, I found myself ready to embark on another one of my "adventures." This adventure changed me, trained me, and took me to war, and brought me home again.

June 13, 1989
Dear Susan,

I really didn't think your little sister would ever be here, but I am. I'm flying in a plane, compliments of the United States Army, heading for basic training at the beautiful resort of Fort Jackson, South Carolina. I always thought if I couldn't imagine what I was doing, then it wouldn't happen. Well, this is happening and I haven't got a clue as to what it will be like! Sure, I talked to Ken before I left, but he's a guy. What will it be like for a girl? I have this gnawing feeling in the pit of my stomach that not even our big brother could talk away. Nervousness? Airplane cuisine? I feel kind of like the first time I went away to Girl Scout camp, but this time I don't think the "counselors" will have cute names like Strawberries and Patches. Yes, Susan, this time I did leave Cuddles, the teddy bear, home.

I was glad Mom didn't see me off at the bus depot. I hate that look she gets when she is going to cry. Instead, I got a pep talk from Dad and a quick wave as I embarked on a 150-mile bus trip that took an agonizing six hours. I hate bus rides. I hope this experience won't taint airplane rides too. Wish me luck!

Love, Mary E.

June 14, 1989
Dear Mom,

I hope I don't stay at this place long. It's called reception. I've been mislead all of my life, I thought reception was always a pleasant experience. There was one other girl going to basic training on the plane with me and when we arrived at the airport, we were quickly herded by camouflage clad shepherds into a flock of other sheep flowing in from arrival gates. We were escorted onto a bus, of course, and driven through the gates of Fort Jackson, South Carolina. We were then herded into an auditorium and given our first briefing (more commonly known as a speech or lecture.) They asked if anyone had any firearms! Or knives, cigarette lighters, or cigarettes or anything else on a whole list of no-no's. Anyone with said contraband was to give them up now and store them, because they say if anyone is caught with them later they will be thrown away and the person will be in trouble. We sat there for four hours and I'm not sure what we did, besides the collection of dangerous property. So begins my life in a haze. I'm just hoping we leave for actual basic training soon, because this place is too crowded. It is a huge room with bunk beds all in a line. If my arm was to hang over the edge tonight, I would probably whack the girl next to me. That's pretty close.

The girl bunked below seems a lot older and she has a bunch of scars on her arms. I don't think I'll ask her how she got them. She's not a real talker. We are all alphabetized so, I better get used to her in front of me and the redheaded Erin behind me. Oh, by the way Mom, I'm no longer Mary E. just McFarland from here on out.

We were issued our linen and taught to make our beds. I suppose that comes as a shock to you that I finally learned how to make my bed properly. Don't think I like it though! You know, I still believe it's a waste of time since I'll just be sleeping in it again tonight. It's just the rules around here. Don't go getting any wild ideas of making your own handbook now!

Tomorrow we start our "in" processing. Wonder what that means? I miss you heaps, Mom. I do wish you were here to tuck me in, but don't you dare tell a soul!
Love, Mary E.

June 17, 1989
Dear Dad,

I haven't been able to write for the last couple of days. Things move pretty fast! In fact, I have already been promoted! Because I have some college, I am already an E-3 or Private First Class (PFC.) I hope this will be a good thing.

I'm not sure what time they have been getting us up. I haven't had a chance to check my watch, because if you are going to shower you need to run to the bathroom as soon as they bang on the lids of the garbage can. Yes, that's our wake up call. I still prefer that to your ice cubes on the neck method. Something good in everything, right?

We get our uniforms tomorrow and head for basic training. Some girls will be staying behind because they couldn't pass the PT (physical training) test. It is a matter of being able to do a certain number of push-ups, sit-ups and a run. I thought it wouldn't be hard for anyone to pass, but I guess push-ups hold up some girls. It has been a whirlwind of shots (sometimes in both arms at the same time), briefings, shots, filling out paperwork, shots and most of all…waiting in line. I now have sore arms, a medical record, immunization record, dental record, life insurance, and contracts. I just hope I don't loose anything. I'm ready to get the show on the road. I hope I'm not wishing for the wrong thing, but I figure the sooner I start the sooner I finish. We have to make a trip to the mini-post exchange for "girl things" they don't issue. Well, I'm one up on Ken, I don't have to wear those nasty brown underwear. I get to buy white. It's a trade off because we'll have to keep the white white. Miss and love you!
Love, Mary E.

June 19, 1989
Dear Dad,

I have officially arrived at basic training. We loaded onto buses with our new duffel bag full of boots, uniforms, T-shirts, and various army equipment. The drill sergeants started yelling at us right from the start. Really! It was pretty much like the movies. "Hurry up! Move it! Move it! Get in Line! No talking! Move it! Move it! Move it! Girls!" The way the drill sergeants say "girls" makes me feel like they think we are all a bunch of weenies and won't make it past the first week. HA!

My theory is to try and stay anonymous, but I almost blew that theory right off the bat. I hadn't taken off my POW/MIA bracelet yet and so far no one had said anything about it. We were standing in the initial formation when the drill sergeant came up to me and hollered in my face. "Are you a sick person? Do you need special attention?" I was about ready to fall over between the electric jolt of anxiety and the breath of hot wind blasting in my face, but I managed to muster out a, "No, Drill Sergeant."

"Well, what is on your wrist then, huh?" His fiery spit dotting the lens of my newly issued glasses.

"A POW/MIA bracelet, Drill Sergeant."

"Why are you wearing it?" bellowed the Drill Sergeant.

Gaining my confidence to reply by focusing on the saliva bubbles forming in the corners of his angry mouth, I drew in my breath and answered, "In memory and respect, Drill Sergeant."

He walked away. He didn't say a darn thing after that; he just went on to harass someone else. For a few moments I stayed tense. I was sure he was going to come back to me. My mind was racing while trying to formulate answers to more questions but he never came back. Aahh, first crisis averted.

Most people have been yelled at for mis-matching their uniforms. We have summer and winter uniforms. The difference is the material. Winter BDUs (Battle Dress Uniform) are heavy cotton. Summer BDUs are a much lighter weight, blended material. Gee, I thought camo was all alike. I was lucky and picked out both a summer top and summer pants, (oh, sorry, not pants, trousers.) Drill Sergeants yelled at people for having on winter uniforms even if the top and bottom matched because, you guessed it …it is summer. Oh, yes, thank Ken for once having told me the story of his inspection where he forgot to zip up every zipper on his flight suit, because I remembered to button all the buttons I could find and I didn't get yelled at for that either. I feel pretty lucky for that because there really isn't much they don't yelled about, but I guess that's how you learn in this environment. Well, I better get to shining my boots before lights

out. No shine means push-ups and I don't think I need any extra ones on top of the ton we already get during our daily morning PT.
Love, Mary E.

June 21, 1989
Dear Dad,

We are in what is known as the Red Phase of training. Everywhere we go, we march and carry a long thin pole with a red flag on it known as a guidon. There are also white flags, which comes next, and blue flags. The blue ones are almost done with training. We watch them march by and know how far we have yet to go and they in turn are watching our red warning flag go by and laugh, "Poor suckers, you haven't got a clue!"

I have been assigned a twin, known otherwise as a Battle Buddy. I am technically paired with Erin by virtue of similar height. Erin is a reservist and will go home after basic training. She has the bunk above me and our lockers are next to each other, but friendships are already beginning to form and I find myself more inclined to be affixed to another girl my size, Leslie Anne. She has the bottom bunk directly across from me. Fortunately for us, her buddy and mine have become friends of the same height too. We have had a natural trade except for inspection when we are required to stand by our official buddy.

Leslie Anne is from a small town and small family in Ohio and she is active duty Army too. She has the most incredible long silky black hair. She braids it and wraps it three times around her head and when she lets it loose, it cascades down past the small of her back. She had to get her hat several sizes larger just to accommodate all that hair. People are laying bets that she will be begging to cut it by the end of basic. I hope not.

Leslie's official buddy, Margaret, can't seem to remember to lock her locker and neither it seems can Erin. Leslie and I have decided we had better try and keep an eye on those two because in the end it will be the two of us getting in trouble for buddy desertion. We have our work cut out for us.

We had a new arrival today, too. A Cadet from West Point. He will act as one of the cadre and is known as a drill cadet. He is the president of his junior class. He rattled off a few other interesting qualifications, but that is the only one I remember. Every platoon was assigned one. This is part of their training, to be in charge of training someone else. Walk a mile in someone else's combat boots, I suppose. He seems o.k. but sometimes I feel like he thinks he's "slumming it" to be down with the enlisted ranks. At least he isn't as loud as the drill sergeants.

One of the girls, Wendy, is madly in love with him. Yes, already. She wants to go to OSC (Officer Candidate School) as soon as she graduates from Airborne school and her Advanced Individual Training school. They would make a good pair since she too has a tendency to think she is much better than the rest of us. She was in ROTC in high school and is what you might call ultra "gung-ho." Wendy has this fantasy that she and Drill Cadet have met now and they will marry when she is an officer too. I guess he's kind of cute, but I don't think it is worth all the fuss.

It never ceases to amaze me how some girls seem to be obsessed with guys even in the middle of all of this. Mom was telling me I would probably fall in love while I am in the Army. What a ridiculous notion! Case in point, even if I was interested if I so much as look at a guy I'll be doing push-ups for an eternity.

I had K.P. today. I had to hand out paper plates to everyone as they came through the chow line because the dishwasher was broken. That would be the electric dishwasher not the living ones. Well, I was instructed to keep my eyes diverted, preferably down when the males come through the line. There is one company of females, ours. The other nine companies are of…you guessed it, males. My neck is so stiff tonight, it makes looking down to write this letter near agony.

I can't imagine getting all starry eyed over these goofy looking guys, fresh with their POW haircuts, but I guess to some girls, guys are guys no matter where or what. There are several girls that go down to the sidewalk in front of our building to polish their boots so they can sneak a peek at the guys. Why bother? There are so many important things going on right now that I can't imagine being hassled by thinking up new ways to chase guys. One girl even let her hair down and was brushing it out down there. The drill sergeant caught her and I think she is probably still in the front leaning rest position which is the up position for push-ups. The drill makes you stay there in that arm locked position for what feel like hours. Even if you are in your PT (physical training) shorts and t-shirt, it is a uniform and your hair must be kept up off the collar. I don't know what got her into more trouble, blowing off the regulation or tantalizing the males across the yard with long blonde hair. Either way, it was a ridiculous way to get into trouble. So, back to business.

I personally haven't gotten into trouble, yet. We have been "smoked" as a whole platoon though. Getting smoked is punishment for being in an especially deep mess. The drills have us in the front leaning rest position or actually doing seemingly endless push-ups, or even worse, the dreaded flutter kicks. The mere thought of flutter kicks makes me woozy. We are on our backs moving our legs in a fluttering alternating vertical pattern until your stomach muscles are about ready to spontaneously combust. Last night, I think they were impressing upon us the sins of our sisters, especially the blonde haired one and we were being smoked in our day room. I swear we would still be there now if it weren't for the fire alarm going off. Some of the girls think the other drill pulled it to get us out of there, but I swear to you, we set that alarm off with our body heat and sweat. The windows to the day room were literally running with moisture and fogged over. I've never been more thankful for a fire drill.

Some of the girls get really mad when we get "smoked," but last night excluded, I don't really mind. It builds my body as well as my mind and it sure doesn't do any good to get mad. I figure the ones that get so mad are probably the ones that did whatever we are getting smoked for.

We only have two drill sergeants (both male) where as the other platoons (three platoons for a total of four per company) have three drills, one being a female. Our female is at a school. Some say we aren't being fairly treated without a female and want to complain to higher authorities. After watching the females drills while I was on K.P. I don't want our female to come back. They seemed to be ten times tougher than their male counterparts. I do feel sorry for the girls that already can't hang. I believe this is one place that is going get worse before it gets better.

Thought you'd like to know some of the "jodies" (songs) your daughter is learning. Some are really gross and I wouldn't sing them if I didn't have to repeat what the drill says. The drill cadet taught us one especially bad one about the McDonald's massacre in California. Come to think of it, most jodies are in pretty poor taste. At least the drills leave the sex ones alone for the most part so we don't have to sing or shout about other women, but then I suppose that is one of their requirements. Well, one of the better ones goes like this:

Oh, hail, oh hail, oh Infantry.
The Queen of battle follows me.
The first to fight the last to fall,
In basic training we'll beat them all.

It's hard to be a soldier twice,
For the Army I give my life.
Oh, here I am in a foreign land,
Spilling my blood on foreign sand.

A combat soldier's the life for me,
'Cause nothing in this world is free.
I look to the sky and wonder why,
Freedom calls and I must die.
It's hard to be a soldier twice,
For this country I give my life.

Everywhere we go as we march along we sing these jodies. It is supposed to help people keep in step and stay at speed and I guess keep your mind from wandering too far or wondering how far! Another is:

They say that in the Army the pay is mighty fine.
They give 100 dollars and take back 99.
AWOL I want to go, but they won't let me go.
OH…OH…OOOOOHHHHH…hey!

You give and extra hard stomp on the "hey" and it's pretty easy to tell who is out of step. This one has a lot of verses and can go on and on about food and life etc. So, if they start in on this one you can be assured you are heading for a long march.

My favorite is our platoon jodie. You really have to wail on it. It would be right next door to sinful to let another platoon be louder than your own. Sometimes platoons will start chanting their platoon jodies while waiting in the chow line just to see who can howl the loudest. I swear even the worst marchers swell up a little taller and march a little better when we start on this one:

Open the doors and open them wide.
The pride of Alpha is marching on by.

Who is the pride of Alpha?
Demons forever more.
Sound off (stomp stomp) 1,2
Sound off (stomp stomp) 3,4
Sound off (stomp stomp) 1,2,3,4,1,2 (stomp) 3,4

I really enjoy marching and we do a lot of it, because it is Senior Drill's favorite part, too. He wants us to win the drill and ceremony competition. Heck, he wants us to win all of the competitions and says if we don't take honor platoon he won't march with us at graduation.

If we aren't having shout wars while we wait to eat chow, we recite the chain of command all the way up to the President or should I say Commander in Chief. We will be required to know the chain of command as well as the three general orders at the final battalion inspection. This is another event we are supposed to ace. Apparently, Senior Drill is a very competitive obsessed man. Did you notice?

Another thing he likes to do before we fall out of formation for chow is holler, "Who is the Baddest of the Bad?" We yell back "Senior Drill Sergeant is the Baddest of the Bad!" Pretty silly, huh? He seems to get quite a charge out of listening to his trained dogs barking or as he calls us, "Ragdolls." Oh well, it isn't as if it detracts from the focus on chow. The food is less than satisfying. We are in and out of there so fast sometimes I wonder if we have eaten at all only the change of the gurgle in my stomach lets me know it gone from empty to nausea.

Before we go inside we break into groups, Active Duty, National Guard and Reservists. Then we have to yell out the last four numbers in our social security number and sign in. During the first days, if someone didn't do it right, they had a whole mess hall's worth of drills screaming at them. It's a little intimidating not to mention embarrassing, because the mess hall is stone quiet except for the rattle of silverware and clanking of trays since it is against the rules to speak except when you are signing in. By the time we leave here, we will probably be able to rattle off everyone's last four!

Well, I better go for tonight. Hugs and kisses to everyone!
Love, Mary E.

June 23, 1989
Dear Dad,

We trained for the first time today with bayonets and I have decided that reality must be hard to grasp in the Army. Here we are decked out in our gear with our M-16s in hand and Drill Sergeant tells us to imagine we are on a plane. Now, I suppose the flight attendant just let us walk right on with an M-16 including bayonet, right? Don't think it was some Army transport flight either, because Drill Sergeant continued by saying a hi-jacker had just grabbed your mother and has threatened to kill her. I found it a little difficult to feel very threaten by a dummy made out of a tire but hey, anything for Mom. I gave my assailant a few swift strokes to the left, a parry right, one grand butt slam to the groin and a final stroke to the head and Mom was saved.

As we continued to learn more bayonet moves, I couldn't help but wonder what it would be like to actually inflict pain on another human. The tires were stiff and ridged when I thrust the bayonet into the general location of a stomach. Would a human body give more? A human would certainly move and present a few more challenges than a tire on a post set in cement, but what else? Would I smell pungent odor of blood? Would he cry out? Would there be a look of surprise in his eyes or anguish? Maybe the hi-jacker would be a woman, a girl like me.

Dad, do you think I would truly have enough strength both physically and mentally to do this? We move from training tasks so quickly that I was able to dismiss these thoughts in the daylight, but now, in these few moments before lights out I have time to ponder these things. I suppose you would tell me that there are no simple answers. Well, that may be, but I think I prefer the situation never arise.

After the dummy exercises, we paired off with our ranger buddies to learn some fighting positions. We must have been such a crazy sight as we screamed our threats like, "YOU are dead dog meat!"

Drill Sergeant would holler, "What is the bayonet creed?"

We dutifully scream back, "To kill, kill, kill without mercy!"

He yells, "What make the grass grow?"

We furiously answer with, "Blood, blood, blood makes the grass grow!"

"What makes the flowers bloom?"

"Guts, guts, guts make the flowers bloom!"

Some girls giggle a lot during our training and I get pretty disgusted with them. I think they should take this seriously because there may be a day we need to remember this stuff. They make excuses like, "I don't plan on going to war so why bother?" Maybe I am confused but I thought this was basic training in the Army not a garden party sporting the latest fashion in camo apparel.

Don't worry Dad, I'm not completely brain washed (yet) I'm just trying to be educated the Army way. Can you imagine me trying to explain all of this to Mom? I'm not sure she would approve of this even if she were the one being rescued! Well, I better wrap this up for tonight. I sure miss you and the farm. I suppose you are ready to bale the second cutting of hay if you haven't already. Baling hay doesn't seem so bad right now compared to scrubbing grout with a toothbrush, but I'll have to tell you about that later as I can hear Drill Sergeant coming. Good Night!

Love, Mary E.

June 25, 1989

Dear Mom,

I went to church today. What an odd experience that turned out to be. It was a group Protestant service and by the end of the service several girls were weeping and wailing and really carrying on! Now, this wouldn't bother me on a normal basis. I think it is important to praise God, and if that is your joyful noise so be it. The part that got to me was the same girls that were professing their faith and promising to be so good were swearing and fighting no more than fifteen minutes after we got back to the barracks. Other girls just went so they could pick up on guys and get their address and phone numbers. They seemed to have taken the service about as seriously as a cartoon bar scene. I just don't like to see such a mockery made of something I think is so precious. Leslie Anne is a Unitarian and they have a separate service, so we have decided to try that next Sunday. It may not be what I am used to but if we go to truly worship I think we will be better off.

Sundays now seem to be a day of rest, a day off. Well, I guess as much of a day off as it can be in basic training. The Drill Sergeants lay low and we do laundry and some extra cleaning. The cleaning is when most of the nasty fights break out. One girl thinks she is doing more than another and vice versa.

There is a pair of girls that do more than their fair share of the fighting. Despite their drastic difference in height, the drill sergeants couldn't resist pairing Johnson and Johnson together. They are like night and day. One is tall and thin and the other short and stocky and boy to they get into it! Their room is way down the hall from ours but we still hear them screaming at each other. Drill Sergeant actually had to break them up at one point for drawing blood. Drill Sergeant made tall Johnson cut her long nails so she would be less likely to draw blood next time. I'm sure there will be a next time, what a pair!

The mail has started to come fairly regularly. I'm not sure if that is good or bad since we have to do push-ups for every piece of mail we get. Don't stop writing! I don't mind those push-ups. Besides, if you get too much mail they let you slide and only do one push-up per letter otherwise it would be five or ten!

We are starting new training tomorrow called CTT (Common Tasks Training.) The tasks are a variety of skills, such as first aid, NBC (nuclear, biological, chemical) attacks, survival under fire techniques, and small arms. I must admit I'd like to know when we are going to start firing our weapons. Oh, yes Mom, don't call it a gun! It is a weapon and call it a gun or anything else and you will be in the front leaning rest position (up position of push-ups) forever. Worse yet is to drop it. We were working on drill and ceremony and a girl dropped her weapon. I thought the drills would never let her up. Bet she won't do that again. So remember, no guns, these are weapons. Mom, I can hear you sighing from here, "What has my baby gotten into?" Ah Mom, this is just training, no big deal, OK?
Love, Mary E.

June 28, 1989
Dear Dad,

CTT training is going well. It is a lot of information to remember, but it is always in a specific order so, if you can remember all the steps you are ok. We have been practicing putting on the protective mask (oh yes, I just got it through Mom's head that it is not a gun, but a weapon so you must learn it is not a gas mask, but a protective mask.) We only have nine seconds to get the mask on and you have to follow the steps to pass. I like the LAW (light anti-tank weapon) and claymore mines too.

People that are especially proficient at a task get to be peer leaders. Now don't let this freak you out, but I am the peer leader on the LAW, the claymore mine and the disassemble and reassemble of the M-16. I guess weaponry is my calling. HA!HA! I suppose I'm o.k. on all of them, because I haven't been yelled at by the drill sergeants, yet. One girl could not get her protective mask on in the required nine seconds and they just screamed and hollered at her. I feel sorry for those peer instructors because the drills are screaming at them too.

There are twenty-three specific steps in preparing the LAW for firing and restoring it. I think they make sense and are easy to remember, but a lot of girls aren't even strong enough to extend it fully. I thank my farm upbringing for making that easy.

Now, the claymore is a little more difficult because you have to check the blasting caps, wire and firing mechanisms without blowing yourself up. Of course, we couldn't blow ourselves up right now with the training ones. There is a step when you are checking the firing mechanism that you are supposed to call, "I see the light! I see the light!" When enough people are practicing this step, I somehow feel I am at a church revival meeting!

The M-16 disassemble/assemble task is timed so if you can't remember the parts exactly, you will fail. The girls will just have to spend a little extra time with it. A lot of them think it is boring, which is so ridiculous because if push ever comes to shove, this is the item we will be relying on for our lives! Hopefully there won't be any shoving around the world!

The M16 pretty much reminds me of the .22. Actually, it is a 5.56mm, magazine fed, gas operated, air-cooled, shoulder fired weapon, that can be fired semi-automatically or fully automatic. How's that for rattling off statistics for you! That's all the time I have for now!

Love, Mary E.

July 1, 1989

Dear Susan,

You wouldn't believe some of the stuff that goes on here! We had to evacuate the building last night and sit outside on the sidewalk for two hours, because some girls were smoking in the latrine (oh, sorry, bathroom for you) and set off the fire alarm. We had to wait for the firemen to shut off the alarm and thoroughly inspect the building before going back to bed. We sure paid for it today. I thought we were never going to finish doing push-ups, but we did just in time to roll over and do flutter kicks. Mind you, this is after we spent an eternity getting "smoked" (no pun intended!) for a girl getting caught in the dumpster! Yes, she was in the dumpster with a boy. Can you imagine making out in a dumpster? How gross is that? Luckily she wasn't even in our platoon or we'd still be in the day room in the front leaning rest position! Really what is the matter with people? Get a grip! Can't they put their hormones on hold for eight weeks? I see girls at church all the time flirting with boys and getting their addresses. They write back and forth and only live one or two buildings away. The dumb part is they use their return address from here and get caught. It is considered fraternization and that is against the regulations.

I would much rather devote my attention to getting through basic training. I'm sure there will be life on the other side. We entered into the white phase. Now, it's a white flag. It's the longest phase. We won't transition into the blue phase until two weeks before graduation.

We are going to start BRM (basic rifle marksmanship) right after the Fourth of July. I really want to do well. Rumor has it, there will be something special planned for the holiday. Makes me a little nervous, special to a drill sergeant could be a nice gooey pit full of mud to march through.

I experienced my first payday. We all got in alphabetical order and had to report individually to the company commander. I didn't even know that's who he was at first. We had to salute him and tell him our names and he handed us cash. We moved over to the next table and immediately bought travelers checks. They have a bad problem with people getting their money stolen. Forgetful people, like Margaret, who fail to lock their lockers are easy prey. Afterward, we went to a store called a shopette. I bought a new watch, because the nice one Ken gave me died in bayonet training. Of course, we will probably never get to go again, because some girls got caught buying candy. Talk about a few spoiling things for everyone. Now, you know I'm no rule worshiper, but for Pete's sake can't they contain themselves? This is eight weeks, not eight months! What a confined study of human nature! Well, better get to polishing my boots!
Love, Mary E.

July 5, 1989

Dear Mom,

Do you know why drill sergeants are like mothers? You can never get anything by them. I thought I would skip polishing my boots one time. I didn't think they looked too bad and I didn't think we would have an inspection. Guess what? I was wrong, very wrong. Leslie Anne said Drill Sergeant wouldn't have dropped me, but that I looked guilty. She said my boots were still better than most. Oh well, down into the front leaning rest I went, guilty look and all.

We had a really awful Fourth of July, but it wasn't for the Army's lack of trying. They marched us over to a stadium where there was a special music concert. They actually let us wander around unsupervised for two hours. Some girls just had a hay day because they were able to talk to the guys without getting into trouble for once. Some people were standing in line the whole time just to buy a candy bar. Leslie and I talked to some other girls that were in the blue phase and just about ready to graduate. They were able to use the phones, they had a pizza party, and their drill sergeant's wife made them cookies every Sunday! Leslie and I definitely agreed we were in the wrong platoon! Maybe when we are a week away from graduation we will get some perks, but I doubt it. Can you imagine, cookies every Sunday? Wimps!

Anyway, back to the miserable Fourth. It was kind of like a Sunday so after we marched back from the concert we could do laundry and clean and such. Then it started to rain and pour and rain some more. They had told us earlier there would be fireworks, but we thought with all the rain they would surely be canceled. They weren't. No one really wanted to go in the rain, plus they weren't until 11:00pm! Come rain, sleet, or snow, like postmen, we were going! Talk about forced fun. They loaded us up on buses and drove us to back to the stadium. They filed us off the bus and through a line to receive a hot Pepsi. Nice try, but a hot Pepsi in the pouring rain two hours after what normally is lights out was not my idea of a wonderful time. Then, the fireworks were late because in all the rain they couldn't light them. Oh, don't get me wrong I'm not really complaining, it is the thought that counts.

It was all kind of eerie. Only a few stadium lights were casting peculiar shadows across throngs of steaming rain-sodden soldiers. Had it not been such a festive occasion, I would have thought we were extras in a prisoner of war movie. So, today we are all a little grumpy and tired, but not really any worse for wear.

We have started training with the M-16. Since it was still raining today, we spent most of the time getting familiar with it in our day room. We had one girl leave since we started to get ready to fire. She was a Seventh Day Adventist and says it is against her religion to fire a weapon. I was surprised, after all the other training we have been doing, especially bayonet training that now she would decide this is a violation of her religion. I can respect that, but it still makes me wonder what her recruiter told her. I kind of figured weapons, especially firing them, would go hand in hand with being in the Army. Oh, well, I'm sorry to see her go. Better start polishing those boots!

Love, Mary E.

July 7, 1989
Dear Dad,

I finally got to fire an M-16 today, even if it was just to zero. We had to start at zero and find our battle sight zero by adjusting the elevation and windage of the sight. We have spent most of the week training how to fire and as a treat one day we watched an exhibit of firepower. It is all going by so quickly. We have been marching out to the ranges and my drill insists we must be first. We were practically running. I have never had so many blisters on my feet. I thought I had quite a few the first week here, but I literally have blisters on my blisters!

Some girls just sit down and cry they can't go on which makes the drill furious, but he has to just leave them behind. So as we continue down the road, they just sit there with their buddy until the trail truck comes and picks them up.

Leslie and I are doing o.k. for now. We had to be road guards yesterday and I thought that was the end of us. A road guard is in front or behind the formation as it is marching. We happened to be in front. When the formation gets close to a road, the front road guards run up ahead and stop the traffic or at least looks as though they would if there was any traffic. They stand in the halt position until half of the formation goes by them. Then, the rear road guards run up to take over until the formation is past. Meanwhile, the front road guards must sprint back up to the front of the formation and the process keeps leap frogging until the road runs out and/or the formation reaches its destination. So, if the entire formation is practically at double time, the road guards are sprinting and you can imagine how tiring it is to be a road guard. Thank goodness, we didn't have to do it on the way back!

During training today, we spent time doing a drill with the dime on the barrel of the weapon to see how smoothly you can squeeze the trigger. I only lost the dime once. Every time you lost the dime you had to do sit-ups. They started by having us do push-ups, but the girls doing the most dime dropping in the first place got even worse when their arms were tired from the push-ups. We were also learning about sight pictures and aiming and breathing and not breathing and remedial action in case of a malfunction. That is called SPORTS – slap (the magazine), pull (the charging handle), observe (the chamber), release (the charging handle), tap (the forward assist), squeeze (the trigger.) The drills were testing us on SPORTS and dropping us if you forgot the steps. One of the Johnson and Johnson pair was having a terrible time remembering the last S. When it was her turn to be tested, she made it through the first letters fine and I could tell she was trying so hard to remember the last S when she blurted excitedly, "You shoot!" They couldn't really give her a gig, because after all it was an S.

The firepower demonstration was pretty intense. There was a team of seven infantry soldiers with live ammunition, who came in front of the stands. The team leader introduced the M-60 gunner, the grenade launcher, and the four other riflemen. Then, he told us they would be assaulting a bunker and vehicle target approximately five hundred meters in front of us. On the team leader's command, they did an about face and rushed forward to the first fighting position. They started to fire and maneuver until they were within grenade range of the bunker and vehicle. They blew up the bunker with a hand thrown grenade and fired the grenade launcher at the vehicle. Then, they set off the claymore. There had been balloons set up at fifty-meter intervals out to three hundred meters and the claymore shredded them all. The tower announcer told us the team had spotted an additional vehicle and called in additional support. No sooner than he finished his sentence, a round from a tank struck the final target making the largest explosion of the demonstration and thoroughly startled us all, even the guys sharing the stands with us. I have to admit, it was so cool! It really pumped me up and I can't wait to fire at targets myself as long as they stay inanimate targets.

We are supposed go to a target range tomorrow. I don't blame them for being cautious. Put a weapon (not a gun!) in some people's hands and they lose all common sense. The drill sergeants were telling us stories about some crazy privates in the last cycle. One guy while attempting to perform SPORTS, observed the inside of the barrel instead of the chamber! He literally turned the weapon around and looked down the barrel with a chambered round and then proceeded to shake it as if it were a bottle of catsup or something! Yikes!

Well, tomorrow is sure to be a big day. I better get a good night's rest.

Love, Mary E.

July 12, 1989
Dear Dad,

Just a quick note tonight. What an experience. Why was I ever born left-handed? We have a little plastic piece to affix to the M-16 called a brass deflector for left-handed firers. It is to help deflect the hot brass from coming toward our faces, but it deflects it right onto my arm! So, extremely hot brass sits and burns my arm while I am trying to concentrate on a sight picture that fades into the fog of my glasses steaming over. Needless to say, I was not as successful as I had hoped to be. Not yet anyway, but I will be. I didn't have so much trouble when we were zeroing because we only shot three rounds at a time, but now we fire a twenty round magazine. I've decided to risk it and wear my contacts even though you aren't supposed to wear them at all during basic. At least then I'll be able to see the target. I've got to figure away to double pad my arm and protect it from more burns. These puppies hurt! Maybe a sock somehow? Well, I'm beat and tomorrow is another busy day!

Love, Mary E.

July 14, 1989
Dear Dad,

I'm glad I took the risk and got my contacts out. No one ever noticed except Leslie Anne. In fact, I thought I was going to get figured out right off the bat. I was standing in a group at lunch and the drill sergeant came up and asked me, "Are you in my platoon?" "Yes, Drill Sergeant." He had a bigger frown than usual and said, "Really?"

"Yes, Drill Sergeant." I guess my anonymous theory is working, almost too well?

I still haven't solved the problem of the brass though. I tried to put a sock around my arm, but that bothers my grip. I'll have to devise something else. It's pretty amazing what you can do when you can actually see your target. We are still marching out to the ranges even though the rest of the platoons are taking trucks. The drill says his "Little Demons" aren't wimps, but other than that I really like this part of basic. Man, I can't believe I just said that! I am curious about something. Do you suppose that when this training platoon is full of male recruits they are still known as the "Little Demons?" Never thought about that before, I suppose it's just another gender connotation like being a Falconette back home. Hmm...things to ponder at a later date, no time now.

We lost another person today. She was older and I guess she just decided she couldn't hang. She got together with a bunch of us and tried to tell us why she was leaving, but I'm more confused now than before. She was saying stuff about drugs. I don't know if she is fighting an addiction or what. I didn't know it would be so easy to get out of basic. It almost like they raise their hands and say, "Ok, I'm done now, let me go home." Although, I guess if you have big enough problems you should go. Well, that's all for now. My boots are calling.

Love, Mary E.

July 17, 1989
Dear Dad,

The saga continues. As I get more and more burns on my arms, Leslie and I have run into another problem. We are short. Up to this point, we have been firing from the prone position, which is lying down on the ground. Well today, we got down into the foxholes. Actually, they are culverts standing on end buried in the dirt. Leslie and I had to make extra sandbags to stand on so we could see out. The holes had covers on them and the drills warned us to be careful when we uncovered them. It is a nice place for snakes and black widows to hide. One foxhole had to be left alone, because it had a nest of bees in it.

I think we are both doing well. Ironically, we are both left-handed. Leslie isn't having the problem I am of getting burned by the brass. She tucks her arm underneath the rifle further. I'm going to try

to adjust like that when we go back out. We are finally going to be driven out to the range on tomorrow because it is much further out. It has pop up targets. The targets move up and down and fall backwards if you hit it. Up to this point, we have been firing at paper silhouettes. See ya later, you know what I have left to do. Yes, boots.
Love, Mary E.

July 23, 1989
Dear Mom,
      Finally, a day without my weapon. I guess I haven't told you about the Unitarian service. It is definitely different. I like it though. It is very relaxing. There are only seven of us that go. It is more of a discussion and meditation than a service. I appreciate the quiet after the week of BRM. We did two meditations with soft music playing. One was to imagine all of our stress and anger as red dots. Calm and peaceful thoughts were blue dots. We were supposed to imagine blue coming into one of your fingers and moving throughout your body until it pushes all the red dots out the finger on the other side. It was refreshing. I felt as if I really had let a lot of the rigorous stress out of my body. The next meditation we did was to imagine our own mortality. Leslie and I decided later that they do that one so you are more careful during the next week. We were to imagine ourselves dead and lying in the desert. We were supposed to imagine the stages of our decay. It sounds gross, but it was only as morbid as your own mind wanted it to be. We discussed it afterward and I was the only one to imagine myself wearing clothes. Everyone else was naked in their mediation. Leslie says I'm a prude. I don't think I could be in this environment. After all, our shower is one big room for all 50 of us to crowd around. The shower is in the middle of the room on a round post with six spigots. If your math is good you will realize that is twelve girls at a shot (because it is two girls per spigot) which means a lot of waiting for the shower.
      Leslie and I are on fire watch tonight. We are sitting up to make sure no one gets out of the door and escapes or that no fires are started in this WWII vintage tinder box building. We have been writing and polishing and doing laundry. We took a nap early this afternoon. We were lucky it was Sunday, otherwise we would just have to be tired in the morning. One thing about fire watch, there aren't any lines for the washers and dryers since it is well past lights out.

Tomorrow we will finish up BRM, for now. We will have a few more ranges, but tomorrow is the record fire. This is the day our drill sergeant has been anxiously waiting to arrive. It will be the first time our points are tallied against the other platoons. Drill Sergeant wants to guarantee our platoon wins everything. He has us study during our non-firing times and we have marching practice right up until we get into the chow line.

I'm not so concerned about honor platoon, it would be nice I suppose but I do really want to do well personally on the record fire. I was disappointed by the pop-up target range we had the other day. They were designed for right-handed firers. Leslie and I can't see some of the targets because they are hidden by trees and brush. It hurts our scores. I can only hope it will be a different range for tomorrow. I think it would be neat to have someone like me from the Hawkeye state shoot a Hawkeye, which means I would hit all forty out of forty targets. I'll do my best, that's all I have to offer. Wish me luck!

Love, Mary E.

July 27, 1989

Dear Dad,

I am a sharpshooter, the second level of qualification. I'm disappointed not to be a top level expert, but with the brush in the way of the targets and a missed shot of my own…well it's history. An unsuspecting little bit of a girl shot a Hawkeye. Drill Cadet said anyone shooting a Hawkeye would get supper at Taco John's. I guess he didn't think anyone would do it. She ate her tacos in the cadre section of the mess hall with Drill Cadet. Boy, was Wendy ever jealous!

Everyone passed the graded BRM section the first time. That is something to be proud of. In the other platoons, some girls couldn't make the limit of fifteen missed shots. They get a second chance to pass, but it doesn't count toward the platoon total. Drill Sergeant was really gloating until he heard the results of the surprise inspection back at the barracks. Margaret left her locker unlocked again. Leslie and I were already downstairs when she left so we didn't have a chance to double check her locker. An unsecured locker is a fifteen point gig and the drill was not pleased. He dropped us all before chow. I thought maybe he wasn't going to let us eat. He didn't even ask us who the baddest of the bad was. He must have really been

pissed! Margaret and her buddy are gone now and have been for about a half hour. I imagine they are being chewed up and smoked. I feel guilty for not having checked it myself, but in the name of self-preservation, I didn't want to be late for formation either. It seems Margaret barely makes it to formation by the skin of her teeth which makes following up after her quite a dilemma. Kind of like a rock and a hard place, isn't it? Miss you all very much. Seems like I've been away a long long time.
Love, Mary E.

July 26, 1989
Dear Dad,
Don't tell Mom, please, but boy am I ever sick. I've caught a whopper of a cold and it has hit me like a brick wall. I am so stuffed up and I'm coughing and hacking. I had to put my Kevlar helmet under my mattress to prop it up because if I tried to lay flat I would cough so hard I couldn't get any sleep and if I'm not sleeping, then my roommates aren't either. Leslie thinks I should go to sick call but I say no way! If I miss something, I'll be held back and I do not want to stay here any longer than I have too. We took a PT test and I had a terrible time, especially with the running. I thought at one point a lung was going to come up! Colds, who has time for this? Worst of all is I have lost my voice. I got dropped during formation this morning and if Leslie hadn't spoken up for me, I would probably still be there! Drill Sergeant dropped me for not having enough shine on my boots, I knew they weren't my best work, but Leslie thought they looked as well as anybody else's. Of course, I had a very hard time trying to ask for permission to get back up from the front leaning rest position. He kept screaming, "I can't hear you!" I would shout as loud as I could, which was a whisper, "Drill Sergeant, Private McFarland asks for permission to recover."
"I can't hear you!"
Bless her heart, Leslie said matter of factly, "Drill Sergeant, she's lost her voice." When I heard Leslie, I thought, "Oh no, Leslie, he is going to chew you up and spit you back out in the front leaning rest position!" Instead he replied to me, "Recover." I was never was so glad to recover in my life as in the front leaning rest position my sinus headache had magnified in epic proportion. As I stood back up, I could feel a gush of pressure moving from my head to my toes. I also have never been so thankful for my buddy, Leslie. Well, I have

already polished my boots for the morning and I think I am going to try to get some extra sleep before lights out.
Love, Mary E.

July 29, 1989
Dear Dad,

Well, I've come up with a sure fire way to get rid of the remnants of a nasty cold, the gas chamber. That is where our training took us today. We marched off into the piney woods of South Carolina until we reached a small shack. The shack had a large front window and two doors, one on both sides. It reminded me of a shack you might find holding a moonshine still as a smoky fog began to rise from a pipe in the roof that could barely be considered a chimney.

As we stood at ease in formation, there was only a quiet whisper of nervous agitation instead of the lively conversations that normally accompany a moment of rest. The whispers ceased but the agitation increased when the training sergeants approached.

"You will be donning your protective mask and entering the chamber from the right door. Once inside, your instructors will lift your mask and ask you to state your name and last four. You will then reseal your mask and you will need to answer some other questions before you can leave chamber by the left door."

Well, that sounds all well and good but the drills literally rip the mask off of your head. I was trying to anticipate my turn so I would be able to take a deep breath of clean air to expel my answers. This theory did not work. Just as I was sucking in a great deep breath, the mask was torn off of me and I sucked down a huge gulp of the thick murky gas. To say it was awful just understates the agony. It was like eating jalapeno peppers while peeling fresh onions from Grandma's garden and wiping your eyes with the juice at the same time you are snorting fire up your nose and down into your lungs.

As I ran for the exit, I was blindly crying with snot gushing from my nose in nasty clumps while drool streamed out of my mouth, along my chin and continued downhill covering my neck and soaking my uniform. My chest heaved and fought for clean breaths as my mind whirled with thoughts of suffocation. As I made it outside, I could hear the screams and cries of the victims before me as the drills unsympathetically bellow, "Don't touch your face!" "Don't rub your eyes!" Some girls puked all over, it was all so vile.

I have great faith in that protective mask now. While I was wearing it there wasn't a hint of the noxious stuff, I was almost thinking they were pulling a fast one on us using plain fog. I was wrong, so very very wrong. This is one lesson that will stick with me a very long time. It puts summer near an aromatic pig farm in a whole new light for me. It's boot time, I better go.

Love, Mary E.

August 7, 1989
Dear Dad,

Welcome to my blue phase of training. I might actually make it out of here! The final PT test should go better than the last one since the gas chamber cleared the last of my cold away. I know I won't set any Army records, but I will do a pretty respectable job. I can certainly pump out the push-ups now! We have had a variety of training lately. Most of it has been pretty fun, which just proves that the Army has implanted a new brain in my head. We had an obstacle course competition among the platoons. We ran along a wooded path that had a series of obstacles to breach, barbed wire, walls, logs, muddy water holes. We had to navigate them in the best fighting ways possible with a low crawl here and a high crawl there with an occasional slide on your back mixed in for spice. Naturally, Drill Sergeant was hot for us to finish first. We tied for first, so he didn't smoke us because after all, a tie isn't losing.

Then, we went to the rappel tower. Oh, did this ever raise a gamut of emotions. This tower wasn't anything like rappelling off the side of the high school building when the Army recruiters came to visit. I would guess this tower to be around 75 feet. It was a lot of fun! Everyone had to go at least one time. We climbed the switchback stairs, higher and higher until we emerged at the top. Some climbed slowly and cautiously as if prolonging the agony of their fear of heights. I admit, I have no great love of heights either, but there was something thrilling about the whole thing. Yet, I found myself creeping nervously to the edge where several drills were assisting. The drills walked us through the process and tied us into our rope seat and assured the D ring was properly fastened. The next thing I knew I was shouting "On Rappel" with answer far below by a buddy, "On belay." Meaning, I am hooked up and ready to come down if you are holding my ropes down there! I was shaking so much I hoped no one would notice as I turned my back to the drop off. The butterflies in my stomach had now turned into birds and then into helicopters as I inched backward toward the edge with shouts of encouragement filling the air. Taking a deep breath, I ever so carefully walked backward off the tower until I found myself horizontal instead of vertical. Then, it was fun! I popped off the side into the air and sped toward the ground. The helicopters whirling in my stomach found themselves trying to squeeze out my belly button while the only thing preventing my stomach from heaving the birds and butterflies out my mouth was me tightening the ropes and stopping to dangle in mid air. The rush was addictive and before I knew it I was back on terra ferma, shouting with exhilaration, "Let's do that again!"

It was all a matter of trust. Trust in your drills on the top, the buddy on the ground and most of all yourself. Some girls panicked at the last minute crumbling over the side and crashing into the wall learning the hard way to trust themselves and the ropes.

After everyone had gone the required time, those of us that wanted to go again had more chances. I even ended up trying it Australian, that is going headfirst! I have to admit, that was even more of a blast! Seemed to take more arm strength to go head first, because you have to use your arms for guidance instead of a combination of bounces with your feet with your hand under your body. When you are head first, your ropes are in your hands first and to stop yourself you have to pull your arm into your chest and to continue you put it out to your side.

I don't know if I am just adapting or what, but today was a pretty good day, but my boots are definitely in bad shape so I better get. I sure love and miss you all, but I may actually survive this!
Love, Mary E.

August 16, 1989
Dear Dad,

We are really on our way out now! We have been on our field exercise, Victory Forge, and we have been to Omaha Beach and back. Omaha Beach was our night infiltration course and what an eye opening experience. It was dusk as we marched down an isolated road not sure where we were going, but by now that was normal. The drills stopped us and began to brief us. "You will climb the cement wall but when you get to the top whatever you do, whatever happens DO NOT STAND UP! I repeat DO NOT STAND UP! You will continue over the wall and low or high crawl to the other side of the course. The rounds fired over your head will be live fire. I repeat, live fire." We filed nervously down a sandy path following the drills. I kept saying over and over in my head, "They are going to shoot at us. They are going to shoot at us! That's just crazy and so unsafe!" As we rounded the corner, there stood a cement wall looming in front of us at an incline with ridges running horizontally for footholds. An intimidating wall bathed in the shadows of the approaching night yet not insurmountable. At the crest, I could see the start of the barbed wire obstacles. We listened to our final instructions when a loud explosion made us all flinch and we were off. I jumped onto the hill clinging and climbing to the top thinking and repeating to myself the whole way up, "DO NOT STAND UP." The rough cement tore at my fingers scraping pieces of flesh away, but all I wanted was to be up and over and out of there. The closer to the top I climbed the louder it became. There were shots being fired overhead and explosions. As I crested the wall with my mind shouting, "DO NOT STAND UP!" I slithered over the edge and into the sand. I began to high crawl with my rifle nestled in the crook of my arms. There were explosions rocking the ground to my left, right, forward and back. The close ones made me wince, sprayed me with sand while filling my nose with a burning sulfur smoke. I continued to drive on, sometimes slipping all the way down on my chest in a low crawl, sometimes the high crawl. All at once, I thought I must be in the wrong place. There was no one in front of me and for a moment I panicked thinking I must have surely done something wrong. Taking care not to raise the height of my body, I turned to look behind me and had my fear relieved by the sight of the rest of the platoon following behind me. The tracers made for some beautiful fireworks but I only noticed them after I had shimmied under the barbed wire and over the burm into safety.

I looked back at the rest of the platoon clawing their way through the sand. I watched them struggling and fighting their way across. In the light of the explosions, I could see some of the girls cowering and I just prayed, "Don't loose your heads ladies, keep low and keep safe." I watched how they seemed so open and exposed. I thought of the real Omaha Beach and how many of them would have perished.

By far, I would say that was the most exciting part of our field exercise. Leslie and I learned how to put our shelter halves together to give us a little tent. We did various duties like guard duty and patrols. At one point, we were set to do perimeter watch, we lay in the prone position with our ears cocked for an approaching enemy, otherwise known as a drill sergeant. Well, we waited and waited as the sun went down and the mosquitoes started up and the heavy dew began to soak into our bones. We began to whisper to each other that perhaps we had been forgotten. I didn't think it was possible. Our godly drill sergeants were not capable of mistakes. Right? Finally after lying in the prone position for over three hours, we heard someone coming. We overheard, "They've got to be around here somewhere." We took that as our signal to reveal ourselves and found out upon returning to the platoon that we had been missing for over an hour. Drill Sergeant would probably swear on his dear grandmother that we got up and moved on him!

Long about this time, it started to rain. I found myself actually wishing for my squeaky bunk. Not that we were getting all that much sleep before, but it was still better than the rain and the mud of our leaky shelter halves.

The morning finally came and we were off to work on grenades and fighting tactics. We moved from station to station learning grenade skills, and then we had a qualifying grenade range, which included practice and live grenades and a skills test. I didn't have any trouble with the grenade throwing as long as I could take my mind off of it being a grenade. I found my love of playing softball to be handy. When I had to aim for a bunker, I just chucked the thing as if I was playing catcher and someone was stealing second. If the idea was to get as far as possible, why then I was playing right field and the ball needed to get home from the back fence. Heck, who am I kidding? It was scary as hell to be holding a real grenade with the pin out of it and try to remember how to count to three before you could get rid of the thing!

Practice grenades still gave a little pop, just to let you know you did it right. We had to go around and collect them to be reused at the end of the session. One of the girls picked one up that hadn't gone off and it popped in her hand. The way she screamed, we thought she'd had her hand blown off. I think it scared her more than anything. She did have a small cut on her palm and that I do not envy when it comes to being in the front leaning rest position. Since it was one of the Johnson and Johnson's, she will most assuredly be in the front leaning rest position!

Some of the other stations taught us how to react to small arms fire, otherwise known as how to get out of the way when someone is shooting at you, selecting fighting positions, which means finding good places to wait behind until you can shoot back with out getting shot. You know, simple stuff like that to keep us alive.

While we were at one station, one of the other platoon's drill sergeant was asking us what our MOSs (jobs) are going to be. She was reassuring some girls that if a conflict should break out, that they would be relatively safe or they probably won't get deployed or they would be in the rear with the gear. She got to me and when I told her she just said, "OH," and then she moved on to the next person. I didn't dare question a drill but, I wonder, didn't she know what I was going to be? Did I pick a dangerous job? That exchange didn't leave me feeling very confident! Well, it's too late for me to change it now, but I will admit, I am curious to find out what have I gotten myself into. I suppose you probably shouldn't let Mom know that little tidbit of information either. Maybe you could ask Ken what he thinks. Well, my boots really took a beating today so, can you guess what I'm off to do?

Love, Mary E.

August 18, 1989
Dear Mom,

Well, our final inspection has come and gone along with our drill competition. We have missed being honor platoon by three stupid points. We won the drill competition and the final inspection, but we just could not make up the disastrous unlocked lockers. Senior Drill will not be marching us through our graduation. It is causing quite a stir among the platoon. Some of girls are really upset about it. They are crying and really carrying on. It makes me mad that after all of this he is going to abandon us over three lousy points. We've done our best. Yet, I have to admit I really don't care right now. I'm certainly not going to cry over it. I am just ready to get out of here.

I was so nervous about the inspection. After all this time, I am still petrified of being chewed up and a spit back out in a gelatinous mass! We had to make sure our uniforms, lockers, bunks, everything was just so. This is where all the studying and facts we had to learn on our downtime came into play. I was just sure I would have a brain freeze when I was asked a question. We all did fine, just fine! I'll admit the whole room held our breath when Margaret was

asked the seven Army core values, but she stated them faultlessly. "Drill Sergeant, the seven Army core values are: <u>Loyalty:</u> Bear true faith and allegiance to the U.S. Constitution, the Army, your unit, and other soldiers. <u>Duty:</u> Fulfill your obligations. <u>Respect:</u> Treat people as they should be treated. <u>Selfless-Service:</u> Put the welfare of the Nation, the Army, and your subordinates before your own. <u>Honor:</u> Live up to all the Army values. <u>Integrity:</u> Do what's right, legally and morally. <u>Personal Courage:</u> Face fear, danger, or adversity physical or moral." Our eyes darted around the room to each other as she continued. Our looks going from dismay to disbelief, and finally, pride. As we all sighed in relief, she just beamed with pride. We were all so proud! Now, it is on to graduation, Senior Drill or no, we are graduating with heads held high and spirits even higher!
Love, Mary E.

August 19, 1989
Dear Mom,

Our graduation ceremony has long since been over and the fanfare has come to a close. Most of my platoon has moved on already. Seems I am one of the last ones to go off to the airport. Leslie is gone. It will seem so strange to be without her after all this time. I thought I might cry when I said goodbye, but we are all looking forward to being off to new adventures. In fact, in all the confusion of trucks loading in one area and buses in another, and those of us waiting where I am, I almost missed her! I don't think it has sunk in that I probably will never see her again.

There were several from the platoon that will be having their Advanced Individual Training right here. They just packed their bags and walked on down the road right after graduation. Me, on the other hand, I still sit here on this step waiting to be taken to the airport. I am the only one in my platoon going to Arizona.

One interesting opportunity this waiting has given me is a chance to talk candidly to our former drill sergeants. When I told one drill Sergeant I was waiting to go to Military Intelligence school, he accused me of being C.I.D. I must have really given him a blank look on my face because he continued on to tell me about sending in the Criminal Investigation Division to verify there aren't any illegal or abusive training practices going on. Apparently, they send in planted agents to assure everything is being done on the up and up. I thought, nope, no one could make me go through basic training again! No way!

Our graduation was quite an experience. We dressed in our best, Class A, uniforms. We were bused to the stadium and then got into our formation and marched onto the parade field. We stood in formation while someone (I really can't say who) made a graduation address. Then I heard "Pass and Review." The band began playing and soon we were marching. It seemed the closer we made it to the grand stands the taller I became. I heard our Drill Sergeant command, "Eyes, right!" I snapped my head smartly to the right with my heart pounding in time to the music and my chest swelling with great pride. I made it! I really made it! I half expected at the last minute Senior Drill would come running up to march with us as if this were a movie. I was disappointed because our Senior Drill did not change his mind and march with us. It was certainly his loss because we were looking fine. I am officially a soldier in the United State Army. Hooaaahh!!
Love, Mary E.

August 20, 1989
Dear Mom,

I made it to Arizona in one piece, barely. What an interesting flight. Seemed so weird to be out in the world again. Everywhere I went or sat seemed to strike up conversation among people. On my flight to Dallas-Fort Worth, I sat between two fellows that bubbled with questions about why a girl would want to be in the Army. They weren't being mean about it, but they did seem to think I should have my mind on other things.

The flight was late getting in and I only had a very brief moment in time to make to my flight going to Tucson or I would be sleeping in the airport. In retrospect, that couldn't have been any worse than Victory Forge, but I was worried I would be in trouble if I didn't show up at the appropriate place at the appropriate time. So, there I was in my high heels, skirt and dress uniform with my ugly old issued granny purse trailing me behind me running from flight to flight. Yes, Mom I was required to carry a purse, it was not my idea! My feet hurt so bad and I actually wished for my nice broken in combat boots.

After landing in Tucson, I was loaded on to a bus and driven to Fort Huachuca. It was so late by the time I got there. The impassive bus driver mechanically motioned in the direction I was to report, but

I had no idea what to look for or expect. My orders were for Delta Company, but eventually I made it to Echo Company. I had no idea there would be drill sergeants at A.I.T. All you ever hear about is basic.

I have already learned a private doesn't walk down the command hallway unless you are requested. At first it was hard to pass up this quicker route to my room, but it only took one example soldier to see it was really quicker to take the second hallway. It was close to 1:00am when I finally got to my room. My roommates weren't pleased with my arrival and as I was putting my belongings into the wall locker as quietly as I could, my dog tags kept rattling. One girl sat straight up in bed and yelled, "Take those damn things off!" I just looked at her with amazement. I didn't know I could take them off! As I finally sank into an unfamiliar cot, I felt so alone, unsure and again in a strange place.

Reveille was at 8:30am this morning as it is Sunday. Sleeping until 8:30am was quite a treat. I thought I was in paradise after 4:30am for the last eight weeks. The day has passed quietly and restfully after I changed rooms. I was so grateful for the change, because it would have been quite a misery living with Dot, the girl that yelled at me in the night. She yells a lot. Perhaps she should train to be a drill. So, now I have been officially welcomed by my new roommates, Betty, Roberta and Keshia to Ft. "We-Gotcha." Oh, great.

By tonight's evening formation, I had found my new classmates for the next seven weeks. All seven of us! Two of my roommates are in my class, Roberta and Keshia. I have a feeling my anonymous method won't work here. I'm sure to be squad leader because I am the only Private First Class in the squad, which is also our whole class. We are in Drill Sergeant S's platoon. He is a short stumpy man with a thick Latino accent. He could certainly be intimidating if he wanted, but he has teasing in his eyes. I think he would be a hoot to throw back a couple of beers with. Not that I would, Mom! Not that I would! Off to school in the morning, wish me luck!
Love, Mary E.

August 22, 1989
Dear Dad,

Well, I was right. I'm stuck as the squad leader and get this, since there are only seven of us in my class, we have been thrown together with a big class of radar guys. Oh, great! They haven't any girls in their job, because it is considered a combat MOS. Should make for some interesting training. Talk about culture shock. I've gone from all girl training to all guy training minus three. I'm feeling rather intimidated by all of this. You know the recruiters don't tell you much about Advanced Individual Training as if everything ends with basic training. So far, the only things like basic are the drill sergeants and PT everyday.

Our platoon guide, the student leader, is a really nice guy from Kentucky, Brad. He is a reservist and one of the radar guys. He's married and older than a lot of the other guys. I'm glad to have made a friend here.

There is this other guy that stands up one and over one from me. Man, does he ever pick on me! He is such a brown noser! Our drill sergeant has put him in charge of the supply closet. So, every time we need any cleaning supplies I will have to deal with him. What a joy, as if cleaning isn't already fun enough, but then to have to beg from the supply miser on top of it! Well, adapt and over come, it is the Army way!
Love, Mary E.

August 23, 1989
Dear Dad,
My first official day of class. We have been going to school, but we have been getting our materials and orientation briefings. Our instructors said not to expect all seven of us to make it. We will be assigned a peer class leader and also a security officer who will be in charge of assuring the safe handling of classified materials. Ha! Imagine me with classified material, right? We actual will have our security clearances as soon as the background checks are final. Another Ha! Me with a top-secret security clearance! I doubt I will be assigned any of these jobs though since I am already the squad leader. The instructors discourage multiple jobs since our class load will be pretty heavy. I am starting to feel like I am sinking into the center of whirlpool, deeper and deeper.
Love, Mary E.

August 24, 1989
Dear Dad,

Guess what? I was made the class leader today. Here I thought I was safe since I am already squad leader, but I guess I thought wrong. To make matters even more interesting, it turns out that guy, Jason, the obnoxious one in charge of the cleaning supplies, is Brad's roommate. So, every time I have to go to Brad's room for squad leader business, this Jason guy hovers around like a bad bee! He is so aggravating, I want to swat him.

Brad is on the third floor and I am on the second. Our floor is co-ed but on opposite ends. Brad's floor is all male. When I have to go up there, I have to shout out, "Female on the floor!" I can't actually go into his room, in fact I can't pass the little crack in the tiles running in the doorway, but I can stand on the outside and get the information I need. It is the same when I go to Tyler, Pat, Dave, or Mark's room. They are my classmates. At least there are study rooms where we can go when we need to discuss things and I don't have to stand in the doorway at length. It is, on the other hand, a little difficult to make sure the guys are keeping their room adequately clean from the doorway. I'm not overly worried about it, they are a pretty good group of guys. Well, off to conduct a study group, we already have a test tomorrow. It is on handling and safeguarding classified information. I guess this is the point where I take a deep breath and jump in feet first!

Love, Mary E.

August 25, 1989
Dear Mom,

Talk about being freaked out! After our test, I was called out of class. I had to talk to the people doing the background checks for my security clearance. I thought, "Oh great, I know I paid all my parking tickets in Iowa City!" Turns out, they wanted to ask me about my pen pals! No, I didn't have to go through all thirty-two of them, just the ones I have the most contact with, Jessica, in Singapore and John, in Greece. They asked me what John and I wrote about. I must have been beet red when I answered, "Well, we started writing each other when I was 15. He used to write me poetry and tell me how beautiful the beaches of Greece are." "Any politics? Did he ever inquire about government affairs?" I had to chuckle, "Oh, no nothing beyond personal life. He is a merchant marine now and we hardly write anymore." "Thank you, you may return to class." I guess that is

another chapter finished in my Army education. I can only imagine what on earth will be next.
Love, Mary E.

August 27, 1989
Dear Susan,

OK, I know I have said this before, but you would not believe this place! I finally got a weekend, a real weekend! It wasn't all it was cracked up to be. Saturday night I was actually able to go out and I hoped to do something fun. We, those of us in week one training, had to stay in our Class A dress uniform. My roommates and I followed the masses to the E-club. There were some of our other classmates and other guys from the platoon there that we recognized and went over to sit with.

Brad was there, and I figured I was pretty safe with a married man. I made him dance a fast dance just to get him up and around. He sure is lonesome for his wife and daughters. Then I danced with some of my classmates, because who else do I know, right? I had an 11:00pm curfew so I left the E-club about 10:40pm to play it safe. I went to bed thinking it was a pretty fun time in comparison to most of my recent Saturday nights. I got up this morning and went to chow, and whispers were flying through the mess hall just like a high school cafeteria. I saw Brad and sat down with him. I asked if he knew what was up and he didn't know so, we ate. On the way back to the barracks, I snagged Chris, who is in the class just a head of me. He knew the scoop and was laughing his butt off about it. Apparently, there is some speculation as to the names of the five, yes five, guys that I slept with last night. I wasn't sure if I was more pissed or embarrassed or aghast! I wanted to take Brad's head off when he was laughing at me! I begged him not to tell his roommate Jason, the totally obnoxious guy, about this. He would have a field day!

Naturally, it was too ludicrous to take seriously, but good grief, it's just like a small town. They think they know what you are doing before you do. Well, I'm off to study so I better leave this burden with you. I do have much more important things to focus on!
Love, Mary E.

August 28, 1989
Dear Dad,

The plot thickens to muddy slop! I was made the security agent today! So much for not having more than one job in all this training. I don't know how I will stay on top of everything.

We have already lost one girl, Keshia. I feel really bad for her too. It sounds like she will be reassigned as a cook and she isn't very happy about it. I don't blame her! Apparently, if you wash out of a school, you get reassigned to the first job on the Army's list of needs. I know they said we would have some loses, but I didn't expect it quite so fast. I better go do my homework, I have some map reading practical exercises due tomorrow.

Love, Mary E.

September 4, 1989

Dear Mom,

What a strange feeling to have an extra day off, but I think I have a great appreciation behind the meaning of Labor Day this year! Yesterday, I was able to go to church. I had been so busy settling in and getting oriented I wasn't quite sure where or when or if I could go. Most of the people around here choose to go back to bed after first formation, but I figure if I am up I should go to church. I also did a little shopping at the Post Exchange. We can wear civilian clothes every now and then. Of course, I didn't have any. It felt very nice to slip on a nice pair of jeans and colored t-shirt. I also bought a pair of cowboy boots. I also splurged on a Walkman and some music cassette tapes. It is nice to turn up the tunes especially when Dot down the hall is on one of her tirades. She has two new roommates, Colleen and Married-chick (I can never remember her name,) and none of them get along. This just gives Dot more fuel for her loud mouth. She is going to the Squint class, the ones that read satellite imagery. I think using her eyes is a total waste of her most aggressive oral cavity!

Today, I have been catching up on some of my studying, but I did take a nice long break and went to the post stables and went for a good long horseback ride. A lot of people have taken off and gone traveling. My two good friends, Brad and Jason went off with some other guys and went to Mexico. I just felt too swamped with homework to go. I do realize the need for a break and as President Reagan said, "Nothing does better for the inside of a man (or woman in this case), than the outside of a horse."

I was able to do laundry without too many people around and it has been quiet for studying. It was weird to eat chow by myself though. It seems that Brad, Jason and I are always together and if I'm not with them, I am studying with my classmates. I think I might treat myself tonight and walk over to the Burger King for supper. It's been awhile since I've had any fast food and it is almost easier to do that then be stopped fifty times by people asking where my two cohorts are.

It's funny how first impression can change. I thought Jason was such a brown noser, but it turns out he was put in charge of the supplies only because he was one of the first ones here. He was here almost a week before me so he had a long wait for his classes to start. He can still be obnoxious, but in a precocious and cute way. Poor Brad certainly misses his family and I can well imagine because I miss you so very much. Well, I'm off to study Electromagnetic Radiation and Wave Propagation. What a page turner!

Love, Mary E.

September 10, 1989
Dear Dad,

Riding horses in the red dusty rocks of Arizona isn't quite the same as at home in the green timber of Iowa, but this certainly has been a wonderful diversion for me in the midst of all this Army life. Today was especially fun for me. I got up, went to formation and then off I went to church. I met up with Brad and Jason for chow as usual and convinced them to go horseback riding with me. Jason said he hadn't been on a horse since the seventh grade. We drew some more recruits as we walked back to the barracks. Chris from the class ahead of mine came with us, as well as Gid, Jack, and Jeremy. They are from our platoon and classmates of Brad and Jason. We tried to get Steve to come to divert him because he has been chasing after Married-Chick, but he declined. I don't know if she has told him or not, but since I always call her Married-Chick since I seem to have some mental block on her name, I would guess he knows. I think that is pretty inexcusable, Brad doesn't seem to have any trouble being faithful. Anyway, he should have come, we really had a good time. Well, at least I did.

It was so funny to see those guys trying get on their horses. It was fairly clear to me, by the astonishing ways they tried to mount up, we were dealing with some fairly inexperienced riders. At least the horses were already saddled for them. I couldn't help but wonder if this was a first for some of the guys. I tried to subtly give some tips and advice without seeming authoritarian.

We started out on the flats, while everyone got their sea legs, so to speak. Gid kept saying, "I can't believe you do this for fun!" I'm sure he was teasing, I hope. As it seemed they were getting the hang of things, we started climbing some of the trails through the rocks. We had gone for quite a distance when Brad's horse slipped, sending some rocks plummeting down the trail. Poor Jeremy's horse spooked and bolted off the trail into some brush. Much to his credit, he stayed on his seat and got her stopped and settled before plummeting down the trail himself. The other horses, but for my faithful Hank, were starting to fidget so we decided to head back. Gid seemed to favor this decision the most as he was beginning to profusely complain that all this sunshine and bouncing wasn't doing a thing for his hangover from Saturday night at the E-club.

Well, Dad, you know what horses like to do when they know they are heading home. It was as if someone fired a shot because those horses turned tail and ran! I was trying to shout at them to pull back the reigns to slow them down, but I was laughing so hard I couldn't get the words out. There goes a bunch of guys flopping wildly on the backs of these horses hanging on to the saddle horn with one hand, reigns held high flapping in the other hand. Meanwhile their legs were flying off the sides haphazardly as the horses dotted back and forth dodging the scrubby brush that was in their direct line back to home.

When I finally pulled Hank up to the sweaty, stomping dusty muddle of horses and riders at the stable, the guys scolded me for not warning them to hold on tighter. I couldn't defend myself because tears from laughing so hard were leaving guilty tracks on my dusty cheeks.

I wanted to walk back to the barracks, but Gid said there was no way he was fit to walk all the way back to the barracks. When the cab finally arrived, we all piled in and they basically took turns cursing me the whole way back saying they were never going to fall for this trap again. Cavalry soldiers they won't make, at least in the historical sense of the word.

On the school front, we have lost another student, Roberta. This will leave me as the only female in my class and platoon. I guess it really isn't a big deal. I don't hang out with Roberta except for study sessions. Still, I feel like there is a certain pressure now on me to do especially well. I don't know if that is a self-induced feeling or if there are real feelings of animosity from guys who can't stand to be outscored by a female.

In our class review by our instructors, I am tied for top of the class with Dave. I don't want to sound like a whiner, but I have my extra duties on top of our class load and I don't know how long I can maintain this pace. I spoke to Drill Sergeant S. about perhaps evening up the duties, but he told me to hang tough. He has every confidence that I will be able handle all my responsibilities without a problem. Wish I had that much confidence in me. Well, off to study C-SIGINT, which stands for Counter-Signals Intelligence Operations. Aren't you impressed?

Love, Mary E.

September 17, 1989
Dear Dad,

We had a PT test on Friday morning. I was really shocked at how well I did! I out scored all my classmates but Tyler. Boy was Drill Sergeant S. ragging on Dave, Pat and Mark for letting a woman beat them. I suppose it didn't help the tensions I was writing about before, but Dad, I really kicked some, well, you know what!

I also aced another exam, but so did Dave. Things seem to be going really well right now and I hope I can hold things together like this for the rest of A.I.T. We were doing more CTT training again, just like in basic training yesterday. Apparently Common Task Training is something that will reoccur throughout my Army career even at permanent party. When we started reviewing the NBC Nuclear/Biological/Chemical section, I was terrified we were going to have to go through a gas chamber again. Testing yes, chamber no. What a relief. Intermixed with all of our schooling has been common Army training, the stuff all of us need to know and refreshers of the skills taught in basic.

We have also been to a range to maintain our Basic Rifle Marksmanship skills. I got to fire a machine gun at the range. Naturally, I was teased about the number of sandbags I had to stand on inside the bunker just to reach the weapon. It was pretty cool. Definitely more kick than the M16. I was afraid I was going to fall off my sandbags, but I maintained! Now, wouldn't that have been a great source of fodder for some of the guys. I can just hear them saying "pansy ass."

Roberta was scheduled to leave, but she has now been held back while they apparently debate if she should recycle or wash out. If she is washed, she will be reassigned like Keshia was and if she is recycled she will just start over with the next class that starts. She would have to start at square one again, but at least you still get a second chance at the job you signed up for. I guess it depends on where your deficiencies are on whether you are washed or recycled.

Now Roberta swears they are holding her back because she is the Commander's lover and he is trying to pull strings to keep her here for himself. I roll my eyes and say, "Yeah sure, Roberta, tell him Hi from me." To which she nervously twitters, "Oh no, I couldn't do that, I'm not supposed to tell anyone about us!" Well now, I'm guessing if she let that little tidbit of information slip to me then her problem lies in her classified information standards and thus will definitely be washed.

Well, if I don't want to be thrown into the wash too, I better get studying. I should probably hold a study session for this latest stuff, but it's Sunday. I need a break from those guys. I found my windowsill to be a nice place for me to study. Seems silly, but it is wide enough for me to sit on with my knees bent. I can crack the window and get some clear evening air washing through my head. This place is spotless, but sometimes the smell of cleansers can be as stifling as stench. I sure miss home and the crisp smells of fall.
Love, Mary E.

September 24, 1989
Dear Dad,

Here is another letter I trust you will censor before you give it to Mom. Poor Mom probably wonders why it is I don't write her. I just don't want her to worry anymore about this training than I know she already is.

Our platoon had our field exercise yesterday. My class didn't spend the night in the field though like the radar guys did. They are affectionately called pop-up targets because they work all through the night on their mobile radars, popping up here and there to acquire enemy positions and such. According to Brad and Jason, they have a battlefield life span of seven seconds. Now, isn't that a reassuring thought? Let's hope they never find that out.

Of course, my lifespan wasn't much longer during our exercise. We were broken down into teams for battle focus training and were all equipped with MILES gear, which stands for Multiple Integrated Laser Engagement System. In real language, it is beeper clipped to your LBE (load bearing equipment,), which is the belt you attach gear like ammo pouches and a canteen to. When you have been shot, the MILES goes off with the most annoying eye rolling alarm.

The basic gist of the lane exercise was to see how we would react under direct fire. As my team crept forward silently using only hand signals, we were doing our best to try and detect any movement, any hint of where our mock enemy was hidden. We knew it going to come from somewhere, but where?

When the attack came, we flew into action but Tyler, who was carrying the M60 machine gun, was taken out on the first hit. The M60 is too valuable to leave behind so I ran back and ripped it out of his hands and went tearing off up the rise. I heaved the M60 up on the top and let it rip, saying, "Fire a burst of six!" which is supposed to be the best way to time your bursts. Unfortunately, part of the enemy platoon had flanked us and I got hit from the side.

When they called a halt, we had to fall back and get our damn MILES turned off. It is like walking around with a stinking smoke alarm stuck to you in the *On* position. So, I came trekking down the hill hauling the M60 with my M16 on my back. You would have thought I was as astonishing as Lady Godiva!

Tyler had been filling them in already about me grabbing the M60 from him, but I don't think they believed him until I brought it back with me. Yeah, it's almost a thirty-pound weapon, but really it wasn't that big of a deal and certainly not worthy of causing a ruckus. Actually, my biggest aggravation was that I didn't think to grab the extra belts of ammo, but then I didn't survive long enough to use what I already had.

At chow, I had to endure all these Rambo jokes and the teasing about leaving the Machine Gun Mama alone. I swear these guys stay awake at night trying to dream up ways to embarrass me!

We had a really interesting class about battlefield deception this past week. It discussed all the different ways the enemy has been tricked by ruses in the past. We discussed how they do it now and all the different ways to make the enemy think you are where we aren't and such. It was pretty cool and a nice break from electromagnetic waves, which are calling my name. I sure miss you and remember, censor this for Mom, she might not appreciate the Machine Gun Mama stuff.

Love, Mary E.

September 28, 1989
Dear Mom,

Got my permanent duty station orders today. I am so disappointed. No Fort Carson. No Colorado and skiing for me. I am going to Texas of all places. Does it ever snow in Texas? I just kept looking at the paper saying, "I'm going to Texas, I'm going to…Texas. You can't ski in Texas…Texas…Texas!" Where in the world is Fort Hood, anyway? Texas is a big state! Brad of course knew he was going home to Kentucky, but Jason hasn't gotten his orders yet. I suppose it is too much to ask for him to be sent to the bowels of snowless Texas too. I am whining, I know it, but I thought for sure just by the power of my will I would be going some place mountainous. Heavy sigh. I love and miss you very much.
Love, Mary E.

September 30, 1989
Dear Susan,

I have got to tell someone about this! I certainly can't tell Roberta my roommate. OH my!!! You will never believe what just happened! I went with Jason and Brad to the E-club, I know, not much unusual about that, BUT Brad left earlier than Jason and me because we were having such fun dancing together, but that's not so unusual either but, on the way home, Jason took my hand. It was like electricity replaced my blood. I wasn't sure what to think of this new development, but I was way ok with it! So, we were holding hands and talking on the way back to the barracks when there was this huge flash of lightning followed almost instantly by a clap of thunder at the same time it started to pour!

Jason started running, leading the way to an overhang of one of the buildings, but we were already soaked. We were laughing about it and I looked up at him and smiled and right out of the blue he bent down, took my head in his hands and kissed me! Aagghh! Not just a little peck kiss, but a long lingering, delicate, exhilarating one. I feel all quivery just thinking about it again! Can you believe it? He kissed me! Oh, it was so romantic, Susan. I swear it was just like a scene in a movie. The rain coming down, we were dripping, him seizing the moment. OH! Just thinking about it I can hardly stand it! I think I could have stayed there forever, but then other people started coming from the E-club and we realized it was probably getting close to curfew. We ran back to the barracks and he gave me a wink as we said good night at the top of my stairs and he went off to his floor.

Of course, what will happen in the morning? I had to write this as soon as I got back here and changed out my wet clothes. What will happen at morning formation? Will everything be different? I hope it wasn't a spur of the moment kind of thing, I would be so devastated if this was a hit and run. What is Brad going to think? What would Mom think? Oh my gosh! Don't tell her! Whatever you do, don't tell her, yet anyway. I don't know, there is just something about him I can't quite put into words. He's always picking on me, yet he is so smart and precocious and yes, cute, no, not cute but handsome. Cute would be for a puppy, but he is, well, not a puppy.

I should try to get some sleep, *try*, I said, not that I will. Oh yeah, guess what, Jason's job code is a 96R and in the Army a phonetic R is… Romeo. AGGHH!! Isn't that a hoot!
Love, Mary E.

October 1, 1990
Dear Susan,

I have good news to report. Yes, I'm loopy in my head. He gave me the best smile this morning at formation and met me for lunch at the chow hall after I went to church. It is so nice on Sunday when we can wear civilian clothes and for a brief time not worry about the fraternization stuff. Jason tweaked my chin when I met up with Brad and him at the mess hall. We, of course, sat next to each other, which isn't anything new, but Jason has this hole in his jeans and I was tickling his knee and he grabbed my hand but didn't let it go. He just held it, aw, heavy sigh. Brad gave us a confused look. I don't suppose this possibility crossed his mind anymore than it did mine, at first anyway. We all have become such good friends here, but there is just something about Jason. Oh this is exciting, but what a hypocrite I am! Here I am complaining about all these women chasing after guys, especially at basic, and I'm no better than the rest. Well, I guess I'm not really chasing after him, after all, he came to me, right? Yes, I can hear you laughing at me. Anyway you flip that coin, it still lands on being attracted to the opposite sex.

A little while ago, I had to go up to Jason and Brad's room to pass on some platoon information to Brad. He wasn't there so I thought I would take the opportunity to talk with Jason on the pretense of waiting for Brad. As my luck would have it, Drill Sergeant walked by, and as I was leaning on the doorframe, my toe had inched over that evil boundary crack in the tiles. He dropped me in the front leaning rest position right there in the hallway wearing my civvies! I was so embarrassed! See, that's what I get! I should just keep my mind in the game and not let it wander onto dangerous ground. Well, I've got to study, but right now I'm wondering how I will ever get my mind on electric waves when it seems my mind is an electric wave.

Love, Mary E.

October 2, 1989
Dear Dad,

Things are looking a little brighter than they did. I just got back from chow with Jason and Brad. Jason got his orders and when I met up with them he said, "Hey, I'm going to Fort Hood, too!"

OK, so maybe Texas won't be the end of the world after all. At least I will know someone there. I should have paid closer attention to the different posts. I just figured fate wouldn't give me anything but the mountains of Colorado.

We have been having some spectacular storms lately. Jason and Brad went hiking in the rocky hills behind the barracks yesterday. I wanted to go with them, but I had a study group to lead. While they were out there a storm brewed up from out of nowhere, and before they could get down it was lightning all over the place. It was sheet lighting and they said their hair was all standing on end and they felt tingly and prickly all over. Pretty spooky. I was glad they made it back safely. It amazes me how quickly storms materialize here. It seems at home we can see them rumbling and seething for miles and miles away. Of course, in this red desert, it's hard to find anything familiar from home. I wonder what Texas will be like.

Jason and Brad have a little extra time right now. They have finished their classes and are waiting to graduate. At times it seems we have been together forever, but other times it seems like we've just been here for a blink of an eye. Jason will be going home on leave. We are going to try and report to Texas together. I wonder if I will ever see Brad again after he leaves in two days. How quickly bonds are made and broken in the Army.

Love, Mary E.

October 5, 1989
Dear Jason,

OK. Explain to me why things happen when you don't want them to and when you do, they don't! We aren't in class this morning. We are in a blackout from a flashflood! Now, why couldn't this happen when you were here?? Around 4:05am, according to the clocks on the wall, the electricity went off and it's 8:30am now. We should be in class! The only time I want to be in class because what else do I have to do without you, and we aren't there!

Dot, from down the hall, is really making me mad this morning. She was just plain acting like a jerk. Just now she came into the room saying, "You've got to take out the trash." She wouldn't listen to us try to explain it wasn't my squad. Oh no, wail wail wail! I held my ground. She was wrong! I don't have time to do other people's duties.

I can see the roof of the E-club from my window. I sure miss you all ready! I can see, too, that people are getting off the buses. Their classes must be cancelled. I hope your flight went o.k. with this weather. Speaking of cancelled, no electricity means no mess hall, so we are stuck with MREs, YUK!

Good grief, Dot is screaming in the halls again. Something to do with Calgon take me away. Well, I'd better go, I should do some studying while I have a chance. There is enough light here in my window perch to see pretty well.
Love, Mary E.

P.S. I just have to add on to this! More aggravation! I settled down to study only to be called out to formation with pistol belts and two full canteens. Rumor had it we were going to fill sand bags for the flood. Wrong! We went on a road march. Senior Drill said he couldn't let us just sit around all morning. I was thinking, "Yes, yes you can! I could use the study time!" After I reconciled myself to the fact that I didn't have a choice but to go, I really did enjoy it. We walked up Laundry Ridge and back down. You know all the dips in the road we run through? They were all full of water. The place where we did of our CTT training was full of water. It was actually kind of pretty.

Anyway, because of my...stature, I was 2nd in line behind Senior Drill. He turned around and looked at me and says, "Yeah, figures you'd be up front." So, he fell back and started walking next to me and asked, "So, you and Stabe got engaged last night?" I, of course, instantly turned red and asked, "wh..what??" and Senior Drill said, "I thought so." Then he took off back up front. I was speechless and everybody up and down the line wanted to know what the Senior Drill talked to me about. Apparently, we were the source of an ever popular tradition called a rumor. Word was, Drill Sergeant S. told Senior Drill that you asked him if I could get a civilian clothes pass so you could propose. How infuriating these people can be! Geez. First everyone has me sleeping with numerous amounts of dudes and now they're trying to marry us off! All the way up to Senior Drill! What's next? Is the Commander going to make us eggs, bacon, orange juice and toast for breakfast?

The squint's Drill Sergeant R. gave us a history lesson about old Fort Huachuca before we came back off Laundry Ridge. He said it had been established during the Geronimo campaigns. Laundry ridge is where the tents of the camp women were set up to do laundry, mending and such. Then 10th Cavalry Buffalo Soldiers were stationed here. I had guess that since there is the Buffalo Soldier statue at the front gate. I always find Drill Sergeant R. to be full of interesting historical facts! Sometimes it is hard to imagine him as a drill with his round egghead glasses and ready grin.

Then on the way back, there was quite a commotion in the underbrush, which turned out to be a wild havelina! I thought, "Oh, great, we have wild hogs chasing us!" I'd close this letter, but the day isn't over yet and what a day it has been so far!
Love, Mary E,

P.S.S.
Well, good night, Jason. Finally, went to class. Then, I had a study hall tonight. Drill Sergeant S. came in and naturally, he picked on me about you. It is starting to get difficult to defend myself because I do miss you. I am feeling pretty lonely for my family and friends back home, too. This place just isn't the same with out you.
Love, Mary E.

October 11, 1989
Dear Jason,
Do you like country music at all?? I hate this place without you. We had to run four miles this morning! I guess it was to make up for an extra day off on Columbus Day. Well, let me tell you about

my holiday. On Friday, Tyler, Pat, Dave, Mark, and Drill Sergeant went out to eat in Sierra Vista for supper. I am including in this letter a candle and "Best Wishes" decoration from the event. Drill Sergeant told them it was my birthday and all the waitresses as well as the people around the table and all the guys at my table sang Happy Birthday to me. I was so embarrassed especially since it wasn't anywhere near my birthday. We got a free miniature cake. I was feeling a little dishonest about it all, but it didn't seem to quell anyone else's appetite for cake.

After that, Drill Sergeant took us to the Pub where he actually drank one beer with us, and then he left. I was thinking about going too, but Pat wanted me to stay awhile so I went to sit with him, Mark, and Tyler and this newbie stands up and says, "Good Evening, Drill Sergeant." I looked around behind me and then back at him and asked, "Are you talking to me?" "Yes, Drill Sergeant." I laughed and said, "I'm no Drill Sergeant!" Everybody had a good laugh and said I should have dropped him.

I was pretty bored without you and I decided to go. I made it a couple of steps out the door when I ran into Jeremy and a crew. They wanted me to head over to the E-club with them. I was trying to find some polite words to say, "No, thanks!" when Jack came along and wanted me to go with him to a party he had heard about. Then, Pat came out and was trying to convince me to go back in the Pub. I was literally being pulled in three directions and all I wanted to do was go back to my room! Finally, as they are still debating with whom I should spend my time, Gid came along and said, "Why don't you all just pull her apart?" I was thankful for his timely arrival and we went back into the Pub, only long enough for him to decide he wanted to go to the E-club. I walked down with him, but when we got there Chris was just leaving. He was looking really down and I asked if everything was ok. He wondered if I would walk up to the Pub with him. So, like I yo-yo I went back in the same direction I had just come from. He got a pizza and we sat there talking until the place closed. I wanted to go to my room in the worst way, but he was really feeling depressed about being recycled, so I just sat and listened to him. Finally, I got to sleep a little after 2:00am! One of my new roommates came in even later than me but I just rolled over and went back to sleep. The next thing I remembered was hearing loud jet noises. I got up and grabbed my clock and it was 4:30pm! Thank goodness there was no first formation on account of the holiday, because I would have surely missed it. I heard the aircraft noises again and realized I was hearing the Thunderbirds at the air show. I couldn't believe I had slept that long, but I definitely had a lot to catch up on!

I watched the Thunderbirds from my window and then called Gid. He was having a BBQ and told me to call and he would pick me up. I wasn't sure I wanted to go since I knew I wouldn't know many people, but I didn't want to hurt his feelings either.

Well, I should have hurt his feeling, because he sure made me mad! On the ride over to his place, he told me he was glad you were gone so that he would have a chance to go out with me. Now, you know me, I normally hem-haw around for words when it comes to telling people no or turning them down because I don't want to hurt anybody's feelings, but I didn't have any trouble explaining the meaning of "just friends" to Gid!

I am pretty put off by a lot of guys that seem to be after *things* I'm not interested in. Makes me wonder who is really your friend and who are those just out for something now that I don't have anyone around to watch out for me. Yes, I'm pretty sure which category you fit into.

I was right. I didn't know anyone at Gid's but Chris. He kindly gave me a ride back. We stopped at the PX and I bought a really good book. I just stayed in my room and read Saturday night. Yes, I am still studying for the finals tomorrow, but it felt so good to lie about reading something that was NOT a textbook, and it is getting pretty much to the point of "if I don't know it by now, I never will."

Sunday was a good day. I got up, went to church, ate some lunch and called home for my Grandma's 83rd birthday. It was kind of hard for me to hear all their fun and laughter back home. They passed the phone around to everyone there. I miss them so much. Today I seemed so far away from them all, so I did the closest thing to home I could do. I went horseback riding for three hours.

Yes, I can hear you groaning. I had my favorite horse, Hank. We rode way up into the hills and we even scared up some deer. Then, we came down and went across the flats and watched some of the air show. It was so cool. We were right on the hill on the edge of airstrip so all the jets were taking off right over us. I gave Hank his head and he just stood and grazed while I watched all these incredible aircraft flying right over us. I felt like I could have just reached up and touched the F-15s as the passed over my head.

I was headed back to my room when I was snagged by Tyler and Mark. They wanted me to, as they say, "perpetrate" the E-club with them. I protested because I was still in boots and horse clothes, but they literally were trying to drag me back down the hall. Finally, I figured what the heck. I did have a pretty good time, even without you. Do I dare tell you that? Of course, I had to endure some of the guys picking on me for wearing cowboy boots. Can you imagine they actually accused me of having an attitude, because I was wearing boots? Apparently they don't know me very well, because you say I always have an attitude!

I ended up sitting at a table with Chris, another "dude" from California and some Echo guys whose names I don't know. We sat and told jokes for the longest time. Gid was avoiding me, which was fine because he was hanging out with this new girl I have dubbed "the Spooky Chick." She seems well suited to Military Intelligence, very shifty. Steve was with Married Chick again and he knows how much I disapprove of that so he wouldn't even speak to me.

Colleen was there too. She says hello. She was her usual flouncy-bouncy self going from one "boy" to the next as if she were a bee pollinating flowers. I really wonder about her sometimes. I didn't approve of what she was wearing Friday night. She was showing way too much cleavage in my opinion. Heaven knows what she was wearing Saturday night. Don't even say it! I do not dress like a prude!

I almost got into a fight with the Dot-chick, she was being a real jerk to me again. She is so obnoxious, and it is starting to wear on my patience! I was good and actually held my tongue. Are you proud of me?

I made the most of the holiday on Monday by studying, reading and sleeping. Then it was back to duty come Tuesday. We had the LRC (Leadership Reaction Course). Gee, I had such a good time. I was on Drill Sergeant S's circuit. We got through our elements ok, but then I got snagged to play the role of POW. I was soaking wet and filthy dirty by the time we were neutralized and interrogated. Naturally, I had to hear smart comments from everyone, even the drill sergeants. "Hey, McFarland, It's too bad Stabe isn't here to see this! He might not want to marry you, but then again, he just might!" "Hey, Somebody get a pictures of this for Stabe!"

Jeremy was there too. He didn't have to take the course, he was just there to help set up. Actually, he mostly sat there and laughed at us. We were doing our best to be uncooperative POWs.

Afterward, Drill Sergeant elected me to go with him to sweep out the bus. At first I thought, "Crap! What did I do?" He quickly explained he just wanted a chance to talk to me without interruption. He basically told me I had done an excellent job at all my duties. He unofficially wished me luck in being honor grade and on my finals tomorrow.

Then, he started talking about US! Yes, Jason, I said us. He wished "us" luck. He thinks we make a nice "couple." Weird, now don't get me wrong or anything, but it is weird to think of us as a "couple." He wanted to know if you were going ahead to get things set up for me. I wanted to ask, "What things?" Instead, I did tell him that we were going to report together at Fort Hood. He said that was a good thing.

Then he asked if I was going to stay in touch with Brad. Before I answered he said, "You know he thinks very highly of you." Guess I'll have to ask Brad about that, but as I you know, I think pretty highly of him too! I miss him, I bet his family is so happy to have him back home. Now, before you start complaining, yes, I miss you too.

Well, I hope you can read this. I know parts are a little sloppy, but I've been trying to finish up here on my bed and parts were written during break at class, and while I was doing laundry and while I was at Burger King. Well, you didn't think I could write a letter this long to you all at once did you?

I really do miss you and I know it really hasn't been that long. It seems more like forever. OK, Ok I'm going to study, for the very last time, EVER!
Love, Mary E.

October 16, 1989
Dear Jason,

This traveling business is for the birds! When I flew to Fort Huachuca, I was running to get to all my flights and this time it is cancellations, bumps, and waits. It's very hard to patiently wait to see some certain Army-man when I know that certain person is also wait, wait, waiting somewhere on another end. I wonder who that could be?

I still can't believe I got bumped from a flight. I didn't think soldiers could get bumped. All I could think of was getting to Texas so I could see you and now I fear you won't be able to wait for me after all. I was sure counting on seeing you tonight. I tried calling your home in Portland. I got to talk to your brother. He seems really cute, but he didn't know anything about your flights. I was hoping somehow we would miraculously be on the same flight so we would have some time to catch up before the chaos of being assigned. Am I asking too much for smooth traveling? After all, the lady in the Fort Huachuca travel office said she wouldn't allow me to travel on Friday the 13th, and I can't imagine that experience being worse than this one. I was sure hoping to take on Texas together. I feel frustrated and alone, but I won't wallow, well I'll try not to.

Believe it or not, I'm actually bored. This little lounge I'm waiting in, here in Phoenix, has music videos going but I don't want to watch or read or even write to anyone, but you. I just don't feel like doing anything remotely productive-like. I would take a nice cup of hot chocolate in front of a fireplace in a cozy lodge after a nice day of skiing perhaps at Mt. Bachelor, Oregon?

The waitress here is hanging cobwebs. She hasn't much concept of where spiders go, but it's an adequate job. Did you ever notice that when you travel you make people start talking? I sat next to these middle-aged guys and eves-dropped for sheer lack of anything better to do. Well, do you want me to loose my edge so soon out of school? It was funny how suddenly their business conversation turned to the military. Of course, if I have to answer the question, "Why would a girl like you want to be in the Army?" one more time I will scream!

Since I have so much time on my hands, I might as well fill you in on all the gory details of my last days at Fort We-Gotcha. It is still hard for me to admit, especially on paper, but I am not the Honor graduate of my class. Dave was. He missed one question on our final, I missed one and half. The whole class missed the same stinking question, but then I missed a half credit on a four part question. I tried to tell myself it was no big deal. I can tell you, honestly, I was really disappointed. There is no second place either. It was all or nothing, and I got nothing.

Drill Sergeant told me that he went to the cadre on my behalf to see if they would award me at least a point for holding all the extra duties. That way we would have been tied and we would have both been Honor graduate, but they said there was no past precedent of awarding points and they were not prepared to start one now. I thought that was awfully nice of Drill Sergeant to do. The long and the short of it is, I missed the question. It was my own fault. What's done is done.

Graduation for A.I.T. sure wasn't anything like Basic Training. We were just in this small room and we walked up to the cadre and received our certificates except for Dave who also got his picture taken, a ribbon and citation. No, I'm not dwelling, just stating the facts! It did seem a little anti-climatic after all that work.

I did have a lot of fun on my free weekend, except for waking up on Saturday with no voice. Not funny, it is not the world's dream come true! I went into Sierra Vista and rented a car for Saturday, bought a disposable camera and toured the country. I stopped at the front gate of Fort Huachuca and took a picture of the Buffalo Soldier statue and I took a picture of the tank crossing sign. Then, I went down to Tombstone and saw the O.K. Corral and the Cochise County courthouse, including the gallows.

I didn't want to eat lunch in the super touristy area, so I headed to the outskirts of town to a more home-style café. Of course, I didn't have a voice to talk with and since I was the only one in there at the time, the guy working just sat right down and shared the booth with me.

He was very interesting with his legends and tales of Old Tombstone, the O.K. Corral and Boot Hill. He saw McFarland on the map case I was carrying my stuff in and first, asked me if a girl like me was really in the Army and then asked if that was my last name. I nodded yes on all counts. "Ah, you come from some might good stock then. The McFarlands was cousins of the Clantons and they told 'em not to be pickin' any fights, but those there Clanton's just wouldn't listen, bet they wishes they had, now from where they is in Boot Hill!" He laughed heartily at his own joke while I just smiled, not having any audible laugh in me.

I didn't need a voice, as the only breaks he took in talking were to get my food and remove my dirty dishes. Ol' Floyd spoke about tunnels under Tombstone for the streams of confiscated booty. He told me where the "real" OK corral had stood which is now in the alley. He informed me how Boot Hill had been moved to a new location to accommodate parking and where to find the "real" Boot Hill. He enlighten me with the story of Ed Schieffelin coming here to start the town and of how Ed's friends told him it was going to be the death of him so he named the place Tombstone. Floyd gave me directions to find a stone monument "Tombstone" in honor of the founder. I went back to the location of the "true" OK Corral and took a picture of Fremont Street to send to my Grandpa, Fremont. Then, I went off to climb the original Boot Hill and then over to the relocated Boot Hill. I had a good time reading the epitaphs and even found a McFarland, who had unfortunately been *hung – by mistake*. I'm not kidding, that is what it said! I certainly appreciated the new perspective Floyd, the Diner man, gave me of Tombstone and if his stories aren't true, I don't want to know!

I had hoped to stop in a few places in the little mining town of Bisbee, but I spent so much time at Tombstone that most of the places were closed by the time I got there. It was fun just to drive through and see it.

Back at the Cochise Courthouse, I bought a book on the local ghost towns and thought it would be a lot of fun to go searching for ghost towns on my way home. So, here I was driving my rented car down these deserted trails that don't even pass as roads. I found a couple of abandoned sights and did a little poking around. At the third stop, I heard a noise. I wasn't too sure what it was so I sprinted back to the car. Some brave solider, huh? Well, I didn't want to rustle up any unsuspecting havelinas or mountain lions. Then it dawned on me, here I am, by myself, in the middle of nowhere, and no one has a clue where I am. I thought perhaps I better get myself back to post.

As I was driving back to a hard surface road, the most incredible moon began to rise. I couldn't believe how big and brilliant orange it was, like a giant glowing tangerine in the sky. I did have to pull over to watch it rise and change ever so gently into a silvery saucer. If I would have had a voice, I certainly would have roused the coyotes with my howling for you.

Well, they are finally calling my flight to Dallas/ Fort Worth, one step closer to you. Hope to see you soon.
Love, Mary E.

October 22, 1989
Dear Mom,

Here I am back at an anti-reception reception. Boy is it ever cold! Is this really Texas? I thought it was supposed to be warm here! It was really warm in Arizona. Speaking of Arizona, you know that tank crossing sign I took a picture of? Well, I didn't need to, they are everywhere here! All over the place worse than the deer signs back home. Who would have thought?

Since Jason had to sign in without me because of all my delays, he was assigned to 2nd Armor Division and I have been assigned to the 1st Cavalry Division. We are on the opposite ends of this huge post! I can't get over how big this place is.

I can't get over the weather either. We are staying in barracks that pre-date Elvis being stationed here! They are old and drafty and down right spooky. Worst of all, unheated! We were supposed to give a urine sample as part of our "in" processing and I had the worst time doing it! I was so cold I couldn't get anything moving. The only thing they had to drink was coffee! I actually drank some, well, one drink. I cannot believe you and Jason like that stuff. I felt like I wanted to scratch my tongue after I took a sip! I proceeded to add several dozen packets of creamer and sugar to it to choke down the rest. Finally, I managed to eek out just enough to satisfy them. As if in the freezing cold it isn't hard enough to pee, but then to have someone watch you to make sure you aren't switching your sample with someone else's. I felt like saying, trust me on this, it is just too gross to carry around pee in a bottle. I will be glad to be assigned to a real barracks and get this show on the road! I do miss you very much and simple pleasures of home, like peeing in private.

Love, Mary E.

November 1, 1989
Dear Dad,

I have been assigned to a Battlefield Deception Platoon. It's pretty cool. Basically, we try to trick the enemy into thinking the things we will do are real. We have fake tanks, inflatable helicopters and other cool stuff. My team has these radio like things that mock radio transmission sounds. Should make for some interesting experiences.

I received my indoctrination right off the bat. I was sent to supply to ask for track tension and radio squelch. To my credit, and not that you will believe it, I didn't completely fall for it, but I was truly confused. I hesitantly approached the counter of the supply sergeant and asked, "Sergeant?" "Yes." At her kind smile the whole confusing mess started tumbling out of my mouth like a stream over rocks. "My Sergeants have sent me down here for track tension and radio squelch, but I truly don't understand what they want, because squelch is a part of the radio and I don't know what kind of tracks they are wanting to tighten and how I'm supposed to get something from you for that?"

She laughed and informed me, that although I was thinking it through better than most, I just officially had my chain yanked. After all of my recent training, it never occurred to me to second-guess a sergeant's instructions.

I'm just glad they weren't too hard on me. I guess I should tell you who "they" are. I'll start from the top down. There is Lieutenant G. from Arizona. I have seen him once so far. I know he is generally in charge of us all, but in my opinion, it is Sergeant First Class W that is really in charge of us all. She is from Arkansas, but she and her Army husband and much of their extend family live right here in Killeen.

The other NCOs (Non-Commissioned Officers) are Sergeant First Class V., she is from Okalahoma, Sergeant K., she is from Mississippi, Sergeant T., he is from Texas, Sergeant R., he is from Puerto Rico and Sergeant E., he is from North Carolina. The enlisted are broken down on teams. The physical team sets up the actual decoys. That team is: George from New Mexico, Fred from West Virginia, and Aaron from California.

My team members are Davy and Bill, both from Texas. You will never guess who will be joining my team next week. Yes, I have it on good authority that Dave, my arch nemesis, will not only be coming to Bat-D, but will be on my team. I think I better get used to him. I have a lot to get used to here.

I had another sort of indoctrination the other morning. I came back from the showers and opened my drawer to be greeted by a big cockroach! YUK! He was sitting there in my drawer on top of my q-tips box just grossing me out. It's one thing to turn on the lights and have them scurry across the latrine floor, but another to have them right in my room and in my drawers. Doesn't seem to matter how clean I keep my side of the room, they are in there.

My roommate is Penny from Indiana. She works in supply and doesn't seem to be too concerned about cleaning. The dust bunnies under her bed have grown into dust dogs. Our floor is definitely co-ed. The neighbors all around us are guys. I guess it isn't really that big of a deal except for showers. You don't want to forget a robe or you will be walking back down the hall in your dirty uniform.

When I go visit Jason, I have to sign into his barracks and we have to leave the door of his room three-quarters open. His roommate Derrick from Rhode Island has a TV, but we can't even sit together to watch it. Since we each only have one chair and one bed, one has to sit on the bed and the other in the chair since it would be a huge no-no to sit on the bed together. I suppose we could sit next to each other on the floor but, I'm not too excited about that after knowing what crawls across it.

Sometimes we meet half way in between our barracks at a shopette. It is kind of like a convenience store, with a little snack bar and video game area. It's just easier than walking all the way to one or the other. We did take a cab to the mall and movies last Sunday, but that would get expensive.

I'm going to take the long Veteran's Day weekend to come home and get my car. This place is too big to get a round on foot all the time. I will fly into Waterloo so I hope someone could pick me up on Friday. Then I will have to leave on Sunday to get back here. It will be nice to see you all even if it is a super quick visit.

Love, Mary E.

December 10, 1989
Dear Mom,

You'll never guess what we had last week! A snow day! I was actually at the motorpool when they said we could be released for the day. I walked back to the barracks along the street just so I could walk in the snow collected in the curbs. It was a crisp windy morning and by the time I returned to my room, my cheeks were rosy and tingling.

I picked up a little bit of snow and pressed it tight and made it into a tiny snowball and stuck it in our little mini-freezer. We had a room inspection today and the Sergeant thought I needed to defrost my freezer. I didn't explain my silly snowball souvenir.

With my old car, we didn't have a bit of trouble driving around on our snow day. I can't believe they closed the base! It was a nice day off for those of us used to snow and ice. Jason and I went into Killeen to the mall and the movies. We practically had the place to ourselves! I was a little surprised they kept it open, especially after closing the base.

Jason and I seem to go to the movies a lot. We can't get away from post very far, and there are only so many trips around the mall you can make. I went riding one day, but I wasn't too impressed with the local Killeen stable. We hope to go to Austin sometime and check it out, but for now, we go to the movies. We go to the ones in the mall and then go to the ones on post. One Saturday, we went to three movies!

I have been trying out the churches on post. They are a hodge-podge of Protestants, but I haven't found one I really like yet. I'll keep trying, but I think it will be harder to go. Sounds like come spring we will be gone a lot. Duty gets in the way a lot too.

Speaking of duty, I have CQ (charge of quarters- the one where you stay up all night so nothing happens duty) on Christmas Day. I was prepared not to come home on Christmas, but then to pull duty on top of it. Well, I guess that's the Army. I better get used to stuff like that happening. I hope you will have a nice Christmas and I bet I'll be home next Christmas. I sure will miss you.

I suppose by now they have strung the lights across Main Street of Fredericksburg. I can just imagine driving into to town with the red, yellow and orange globes twinkling on the shiny green garlands as they gently swing back and forth over our heads as we drive down the street. Of course, we aren't allowed to put up a Christmas tree, so I cut one out of construction paper and taped it to the wall. It works and is definitely more festive than nothing. I better stop before I make myself even more home sick. I love you.
Love, Mary E.

December 31, 1989
Dear Dad,

I'm writing this on my brand new toy. It took about a whole paycheck, but I think it should prove to be well worth it. Besides, I really like it. In this age of computer everything, I thought I'd get a little in the craze. I don't need all the extras of a computer, so I got a word processor. I will leave the computer business to my own personal computer wizard, Jason.

I have decided to start taking correspondence courses from the University of Iowa. I would really like to finish what I started and get my bachelor's degree. I thought this machine would really come in handy for homework assignments.

I also want on write a paper about women in the Army. Three sergeants I work with are 11B (11 bravo's are infantrymen.) Anyway, these hard core Army boys are under the impression that women should not be in the Army because they can get pregnant. I went to the library and checked out every possible book I could and I intend on writing one big paper. The next time they start to hassle me – boom- I'll slap down some hard core facts! I could really get them on harassment charges, but no use making them madder than they already are at women.

Well, Christmas was...different. If there was a candlelight church service somewhere, I couldn't find it. It felt like there were a lot of holes in this Christmas. I really enjoyed being able to talk to almost everyone on the phone. I guess family is family even if I am way down in the dregs of Texas. I put the packages everyone sent on the floor under my construction paper Christmas tree. Jason and I exchanged gifts on Christmas Eve since I was to be on twenty-four hour duty on Christmas.

I got Jason a book on motorcycle racing. He likes motorcycles like I like skiing. Jason got me a big stuffed monkey for Christmas. It's really soft, but it has so much hair that it is a static electricity nightmare! He says it is to keep me company when he is gone, and it does sound like he will be gone a lot this coming year.

Looking at the bright side, I sure didn't have to worry about over-eating this holiday season. Jason went to his sergeant's for Christmas dinner since I was stuck on duty. He brought me a plate of food. All day my mouth was watering for the taste of good Christmas food, but much to my surprise and yes, disappointment, it was a Korean Christmas dinner. It was so thoughtful, but I did miss the turkey, mashed potatoes and good Iowa corn. It seems silly to think Christmas isn't quite Christmas without mandarin orange Jell-O with the cute little pastel marshmallows.

Jason has something up his sleeve for tonight, but he won't tell me. He's much better at that sort of thing than I am. In fact, the presents probably wouldn't have survived until Christmas Eve if it wasn't for him. He doesn't give out hints either! I kept asking for hints on my present and he told me it was a mouth organ! Imagine that, Dad! I told him about how you always told us our presents were mouth organs and what does he do, but use it on me too!

Well, I guess that is all for this year. I wish you and all the family a Happy New Year and the best 1990 possible. Wish I could be there! Love and miss you all very much!
Love, Mary E.

January 9, 1990
Dear Mom, Grandma and Grandpa,

I had a whole two-page letter all written out when Dad's wife, Linda, called. Bad news. It made that letter seem rather insignificant. So, I turned the machine off and will start another letter.

I'm sure by the time you get this you'll have heard for yourselves about Akio, the Japanese exchange student staying with Dad and Linda, who was hit and killed by a milk truck Saturday morning. I really don't know any details myself. I was pretty speechless when I received the call. What an awful tragedy. Death is sad, but especially when one is so young. He was sixteen, with a life of promise ahead.

I was on CQ when she called.

Love, Mary E.

January 20, 1990
Dear Mom, Grandma and Grandpa,

Hello Uncle Jim! I hope you are having a nice stay with Mom, Grandma and Grandpa!

We have put in for ten days of leave for my birthday. Hopefully we will be approved. Yes, I said we, because Jason will be coming with me.

Jason and I went to the movies Saturday night and we are still in a heated debate about it. We saw <u>Born on the 4th of July.</u> It is a movie about soldiers returning home from the Vietnam War and how the country treated them. Jason and I share very similar opinions, but mine are just more idealistic than his.

This week was pretty slow. It had been really warm until Friday. Naturally, Friday was the day we had to wash all the vehicles in the motor pool. I had to wash three big 2-½ ton trucks along with one regular sized blazer type truck. I was soaked to the bone and nearly frozen stiff. I sure would have enjoyed a bathtub!

Love, Mary E.

February 20, 1990
Dear Mom, Grandma and Grandpa,

What do you call a Polled Hereford in drag? A Dairy Queen. Don't worry, I didn't laugh either. I was bombarded with this – joke – today. I had to explain to Jason that Polled Herefords are beef cattle and the polled meant they were naturally hornless. I went on explain that you milk dairy cows and that the black and white ones are Holsteins not Olesteins. So goes the "countryfying" of Jason.

Thirty days and counting until leave. The excitement is mounting daily. I can't wait. It's been ages since I've been home for my birthday. I wish I could have a longer time span though. I wish Jason and I could take thirty whole days go to Iowa and continue on a cross country trip to explore the wonders of Oregon and everything in between. Oh well, patience is a virtue, right?

I have been sent to a mechanic school for the last two weeks. It has been an interesting sidetrack from normal duties. It is important for us to be self-sufficient in Battlefield Deception because we are out on our own a lot. So one more dirty day of mechanic school, then a test, a cleaning day and then graduation. I don't think I have ever been so dirty. I know you find that hard to believe but, really, EVER! I ruined a set of BDUs, but I kept wearing the same ones. Yes, I washed them every night. Grease, battery acid, rips, you name it!! I do really feel like I have learned, but remembering and using will be another story.

Well, that's about all for now. I can't wait to see you!
Love, Mary E.

March 3, 1990
Dear Grandma,

I hope you don't mind this is written on the back of a Fort Hood map. I'm in my truck–again. I just hate wasting time by just sitting and waiting so I dug this map out of the glove box. Funny, I have this nice word processor sitting at home, but I still seem to end up writing most of my letters by hand and mostly from the seat of this truck.

Looks as if this truck and I are destine to become good friends. I still can't believe I was honor graduate at Mechanic School! Perhaps I have chosen the wrong field and I should have become a mechanic in the first place. Nah, I do think this Bat-D stuff is pretty cool, a lot of work, but pretty cool.

I had to go to an Army physical. They check your cholesterol, HIV and other blood things, urine, eyes and hearing. Such a lot of fun! My hearing is still good, but they say my eyes are worse. I think it was the machine. Without my glasses I have 20/400 vision and she said with my glasses I was 20/70. I'm going to have them re-checked because I know I see better than that. I was 20/20 when they checked at basic. I don't think even my eyes would go that bad that fast.

Well, that is about all for now. Nothing much to write because there doesn't seem to be much going on here just duty, duty, duty and very little time for play. I can't wait to come home on leave! I am so excited about bringing Jason home to meet all of you!
Love, Mary E.

April 8, 1990
Dear Susan,

I trust you had a good birthday. Hope you did even though I wasn't there to harass you about being yet another year older! It was sure good to see you, but I wish we could have stayed for your birthday too!

Our drive home was certainly different than our drive up! I can hardly believe that I have traded good reliable "Frenchie" the 1966 Plymouth Valiant for a deuce coupe Toyota MR2. Times, they are a changin'.

I hope you liked Jason when you finally got to meet him. It seemed like such a fast and furious trip home. I can't believe Dad took Jason to the meat locker! Well, I guess Dad must have liked him, because he brought him back whole! I suppose it goes without saying, the best part of the whole trip was my birthday. It was so cool when Jason proposed to me right there in Grandma's garden. It was so completely romantic with him down on one knee, hand over heart. Then, making such a pronouncement to you all at my party. Aw, don't you just love him? I do!

You know, Susan, I am so glad you live thirty miles away from Mom and Dad. I know all my letters get passed around to the family. Mom reads hers right at Grandma and Grandpa's. Dad is very good about taking my letters down to Grandma's and over to Ken's, but I feel I can just write you. It is a great relief to me since there are some things I just don't want Mom or Dad and everyone else to know. This is one of them.

Jason and I have decided to live together. We found a little studio apartment not far from post. It's so small, but I think it's just perfect. It is already furnished by rented furniture, but we had the option to continue the "contract" for it. Oh, it is so cute! The best part is it's cockroach free!

I can just hear the Grandmas saying we are "living in sin" but it really isn't like that at all. It's not like we aren't engaged and going to get married after all, but our time together is so limited that we want to make the best of it when we can. At the barracks, we are still required to keep the door three-quarters way open and we can't even sit together. I totally understand the policies against fraternization, but a person does need their space and personal time too.

I'll admit, we have spent way too much money on hotel rooms! I know, doesn't that sound awful? It's like we are some sort of star-crossed lovers, but really it is just so we can be together and do simple things like cuddling while we watch TV. Doesn't sound too torrid, does it?

I drug my laundry down to Jason's barracks when we got back so we could spend that time together. We were talking about life beyond the Army. We decided we are probably destined to an "average" life. We will probably have a white house, two kids, and a dog named Shep. Jason will work for some company and he thinks I should be a teacher or, get this, a librarian! I guess Grandma must be rubbing off on me. I laugh, but that doesn't seem so awful.

After finishing the laundry, we went out for supper. Jason had this strange expression on his face so I asked, "What's up?" He broke into a smile and said, "There are two types of women. The ones you want to marry and the ones that are so gook looking you just want to lick their make-up off!" I giggled as my face washed red, although I wondered where exactly I fit into those categories.

Reaching across the table for my hand, he continued, "I never thought it was possible to find both types of a woman all wrapped up in one. You are so beautiful. With you, thinking about being married isn't scary anymore." He raised my hand to his lips and kissed it. Wow, I would follow him to the ends of the earth. I think I really truly would.

It is so easy to be with him. We can act like teenagers-snickering, making jokes, picking on each other, but we have serious times too. We can talk about anything and everything. We can talk for hours and not even realize that time is passing. I feel like we have been best friends all our lives.

When it comes time for us to go back to our barracks it is just miserable. Our days are so busy and we are gone so often, that it just seems like torture to leave him. So, moving off post together seemed like the best answer, the only answer.

So, you know our secret. I hope you don't think it is being dishonest. I'm just ready to share my life with Jason, legally or not. Thanks for listening to me. I love you and already miss you terribly. Love, Mary E.

April 22, 1990
Dear Susan,

Not even sure if you have received my last letter while I am writing this one. I can't believe I am married! I must admit I was a little disappointed in everyone's reaction when we called you all on Sunday to tell the news. I expected gasps or shock or something. To quote Dad, "Well, I'm not too surprised." I am so glad we decided to get married. It didn't feel right to either of us to be living together without being married.

I will always remember the officiating Judge. He kept saying over and over to me, "You, You are in the Army?" I found a pretty white Easter dress at the mall and actually curled my hair, but I didn't think I looked that out of character.

I well remember your wedding and all the hubbub. Not that it wasn't exciting and emotional and a wonderful event, but you know I would have had a terrible time being the center of attention. Jason and I got up on Friday morning after appropriately sleeping in, after all, it was weekend pass day. We ate a little breakfast and watched a little TV. It was almost like any other Saturday. Then after lunch we got dressed up, got in the car, drove to the courthouse, and at about 3:15pm we were married. It was quiet and romantic (to me.)

We had supper with our friend, Steve. We had a good laugh that now Jason could drink off post because now I was his "legal guardian." It certainly doesn't feel like I am older than he is. At nineteen, he seems like such an old soul to me.

We plan on taking a more honeymoon-kind-of-trip later around Memorial Day, but we took a short trip on Saturday to Austin and went through a cave and ate at this very nice restaurant at the top of a hotel call Foothills. We went to the mall and a movie on Sunday and then decided to call everyone. We were going to keep it secret since we still plan on having our church wedding on December 31st, but then I got to thinking of the grandmas. So, we spilled our beans,

I'm glad we did because news like this would have been too hard to keep quiet anyway.

This morning was pretty much back to business as usual, except for me having to request time to get the paperwork to officially change my name and ID. I can't change my dog tags or tags on my uniform until the Army officially recognizes we are married.

We would have liked to been married in a church, but the chaplain said we would have to wait for twelve weeks. I don't think I would have felt comfortable waiting that long. I was worried I wouldn't feel really married having a Judge instead of a Pastor, but, Susan, I love him so much just being together holding hands, speaking our vows, I feel completely married.

We couldn't get any more time off than a pass, and we couldn't take leave since Jason will be going to the field soon. Even being married won't keep us from being separated by the Army, but at least when we are together we will have our own space and our own time. Will you still be my matron-of-honor in December?

Love, Mary E.

May 13, 1990
Happy Mother's Day, Mom!

I do wish we could be near you today. You will be glad to know we have found a very nice church just right down the street. We really enjoy it and the Pastor used to be in the Navy. He is certainly filled with the Holy Spirit and each sermon is truly an event!

They are having a revival all this week, but I have been assigned several weeks of funeral detail, so I doubt I will be able to go to any of it. If anyone in the state of Texas passes away and requests military rights, we go to be the twenty-one gun salute. My feet are getting so sore from the low quarter dress shoes I have to wear. I truly miss my good old well broken in boots! I have been to several funerals so far. Texas is a big state! It has been interesting to see more of the state, but it has all been out the window of a van.

I sure miss you, but I will be coming home for a little visit in June so I will see you soon!

Love, Mary E.

June 4, 1990
Happy Birthday, Dad!

I hope you have a great day. We sure had a nice Memorial Day. I guess you could call it our honeymoon, because we took advantage of the extra day off and traveled down to San Antonio. We went to the Alamo and a huge cave. We stayed in a fancy hotel and found the coolest little jazz place along the Riverwalk. It was very nice and very unlike the Army. I had to introduce Jason to the merits of your well taught lesson of stopping at all historical markers along the way. Jason also laughs at me for checking out all the crops as we drive. The crops of Texas are certainly different from our corn and soybeans. Can't wait to see you and your crops soon.

Love, Mary E.

June 6, 1990
Happy Birthday, Mom!

Not much longer now and I'll be sneaking back home for a quick visit. I am pretty excited to see all of my high school classmates for our first reunion. Yes, Mom, I am excited to see you too! I am disappointed Jason won't be able to come. He will be on another field exercise. We keep missing each other. He goes out, I come in. Bad timing, but I guess that is to be expected in two different Divisions.

The last time I was on a field exercise I took the driver's exam for a HUMV. Davy told me you can't sink a hummer, but while make a river crossing, I got the thing stuck. Boy, did I ever hear the cracks about women drivers! We had to hike back to the Motorpool for our big truck to pull it out. After all that, we still had to do our mission. When we finally stopped for the night, the coyotes were so loud, I swear they were in my little shelter with me. Also that night, an MP was run over by a truck and killed at a checkpoint. Now, the MPs at the checkpoints have to pop chemical lights at night so we can see them better. In Bat-D, we set-up our sites in the cover of darkness, but then we can pull back to a safe location and settle in for the night. Jason, on the other hand, works all night long. Jason said the last time he was out his team accidentally ran over an armadillo with the tracked vehicle. It guess it made quite an explosion with it's armor. Poor thing. Jason and his guys come home so tired, but then, I guess we all do.

I sure look forward to seeing you soon. I wish it could be longer, but I guess we take what we get.

Love, Mary E.

July 4, 1990
Dear Mom,

What a show the 1st Cav put on for the Fourth of July! The Troopers on their horses gave quite a spectacular riding show, and later that night the fireworks were great. I was very impressed. I was especially glad that Jason and I were together.

It's turning into quite a summer with all of our field exercises. We seem to see each other few and far between. I am so thankful that our apartment is so small. I can be in bed and see the whole place. I don't care if I am supposed to be some tough soldier, I prefer it when my husband is home and I am not all alone.

So, has Grandma stopped going on about me and my cooking yet? I can't help it that I spent more time fixing fence with Dad and Grandpa than I did in a kitchen. Hey! At least I am trying. I know I thoroughly shocked her when I called asking how to cook chicken and she found out I had "set-up housekeeping" without any flour in the house. Yes, macaroni and cheese, popcorn and frozen pizzas are still my staples when Jason is gone. I have been trying to get better at cooking, but thank goodness for delivery pizza and Chinese food when my creations are a disaster!

I sure miss you. It was so nice to see you, but so hard to say goodbye again. Seems I keep having to say more and more goodbyes the older I get. I don't know that I like that!
Love, Mary E.

July 29, 1990
Dear Dad,

I'm not going to have a chance to write for about thirty days. I will be going on a joint FTX (field training exercise) with the Air Force. We will be setting up our decoys all over the state of Texas. There will also be teams setting up real equipment. The Air Force will fly recon, and then Intel has to decide which are live and which are Memorex. Should be kind of cool. I will get to see a lot of Texas this way.

I'm not very happy about being away from Jason so long. He has been gone two weeks on his own FTX and won't come back until three days after I am gone. We leave a lot of notes for each other. It sure makes me appreciate the time we do have together. I look forward to some down time come winter. I miss our moviefests, our little trips to Austin and just plain being together. We are anxious to put our leave in for Christmas, Wedding and New Year's. I hope it will be approved, but I can't think of any reason why it wouldn't be. I think wedding plans are going pretty well. Thanks for putting our deposit down on the reception hall for us.

Well, I guess I better get packing. Maybe I'll be able to drop you some postcards from an oil well or something.

Love Mary E.

August 5, 1990
Dear Dad,

Our FTX has been cancelled. I can't say anymore than, watch the news.

Love, Mary E.

September 29, 1990
Dear Dad,

It sure seems like a long long time since I have been able to write home. It's good thing I tucked some extra paper in my map case before we left. We are currently stranded in a small roadside café with an attached garage somewhere in southern Texas. We are supposed to be on a vehicle convoy to the port in Houston where all of this equipment will be shipped to Saudi Arabia for Desert Shield. Well, my truck overheated and the brakes were getting very soft so we were forced to stop. My floorboard was getting so hot that I had to start using a board to push the pedal. I have my Army summer "jungle" boots on and there is a metal plate in the bottom of them that was really absorbing the heat off of the pedal and floorboards. I am starting to feel a little insecure about being in the Saudi Arabian Desert in these poor old 1966 vintage trucks. If they can't endure the Texas heat, how will they be able to endure Saudi?

When we left this morning it was pouring, I had my raingear with me, thankfully. My driver's side window won't roll up, the crank mechanism has been broken long before I was the driver, but the part has yet to come. The mechs keep telling me it has been ordered! I don't think it matters now. I felt even worse for Sergeant T and Davy. The cab canopy of their truck ripped and they had to tear it the rest of the way off because it was flapping so bad. Basically, they are now driving a convertible with the top down all the time. So, they were getting soaked this morning and now that the sun is out, they are getting fried without any shade.

I suppose I should thankful for the opportunity for a rest. I considered breaking into the stash of books that I packed under the seat of my truck, but thought perhaps I should write home instead. I have the seat so carefully stuffed I'm not sure I'll ever be able to put it back once I take one thing out. We sure have been on the go seven days a week for the last seven weeks.

I was standing in the motor pool rolling camouflage net when we first heard about the invasion of Kuwait. It seemed so far away, so disconnected from us. Why should we be concerned about this nut-ball? We packed our trucks and drove them to Bergstrom Air Force Base for our joint exercise, but when we got back to post, we found we had been put on alert. So we had to turn around immediately and go back to Austin and bring our trucks home. We knew we wouldn't be leaving on our joint exercise.

As we were unloading the trucks, the conversation naturally turned to the Persian Gulf. Dave kept saying, "We're going! We're going! We are third on the list and the 82nd is on its way and 101st is loading up!" I said, "If we go to Saudi Arabia, I'll eat my shorts!" Well, they say there are these things called edible underwear, do you suppose there are edible shorts?

I knew it was getting serious when they pulled Jason in from the field. In fact, all field exercises were cancelled. When they called to tell me I was going, I got scared, very scared. All I knew was I was going-not when or how long, but I was going and I couldn't tell a soul. I'm sorry I couldn't tell you right away, but you understand that there will be a lot of things I won't be able to tell you right away, if ever. I will always remember what you said when I finally told you, "I expected this from my son, but never my daughter." I have to admit I am still pretty scared. I've never been to war before and it certainly does not ease my mind knowing that Jason is going too!

If we ever get these vehicles to the port, we are supposed to have time to pack and take care of personal issues before we leave. Jason is probably already at the port since he is driving a Hummer, lucky dog. He may have to take care of everything on his own if I don't get this thing moving! We have had just one day off since this all started in August. That hasn't given us much time to get our affairs in order. I still don't know what we should do with the apartment, our stuff, Jason's motorcycle, our car?

The Army has been slow to recognize the problems of a dual military couple. I can't imagine how much harder this would be with kids! Hopefully, we will have enough time to figure all this out! Maybe it will be me that has to do it all on my own. There aren't any females being tasked to go on the ship with the vehicles, but I am afraid they will assign Jason. I am starting to feel like Grandma doing all this worrying. Well, it looks like we are actually ready to haul. Wish me luck!

Love, Mary E.

October 8, 1990
Dear Dad,

It's official, we have been deployed. We finally got the trucks to the port. It took us 15 hours to go 250 miles, but they are there. I'm just glad we didn't have to stick around to put them on the ships!

We finally got the apartment stuff figured out as well. I am very grateful for your help in solving some of the problems. Everything in the apartment is packed and the Army is supposed to send someone to store it for us. The furniture rental place will be picking their items up as well. Our stuff was on the south side of the living room and the rental was on the north side and in the bedroom. Oh man, I hope they don't screw it up!

I went off and forgot my canteen in the freezer, but we had plenty of time for Sergeant E to drive me back to get it. I was kind of glad, because I could double check everything was where it should be and everything was shut off. I'm sure going to miss that little place.

We made arrangements with our property manager for you to do our apartment check out. It is reassuring to me that you will be able to check that nothing was left behind. It seems like a long trip for you to come all the way down to Texas, but I certainly appreciate that you are going. I hope you won't have any trouble closing out the apartment or taking the car back to Iowa with you. We didn't have any problems getting Jason's motorcycle into storage. It was just a very long wait. Imagine that, waiting.

We are on the last leg our journey now. Our departure date kept getting pushed back and I began to think that we wouldn't have to go. Part of me thought that this was just all a bad dream, but those beliefs have been shattered now that we are on this plane. Here we go.

I was hoping I'd get to fly over with Jason, but I didn't know for sure until he was sitting here next to me. He had to go with his unit and me with mine. We still had to wait most of the day for a flight. We had an official send-off in a gym, and I caught a glimpse of

Jason and he of me. I was hoping there was some way we could sit together. When the call came to load the buses, they separated people by smokers and non-smokers, so we jumped at the chance to load the bus together. Then as we boarded the plane, I had the stupid fear, what would happen if the row ended and I would be forced to start a new row on the opposite end of Jason! I didn't need to worry.

We have been sleeping most of the way over. We are all absolutely exhausted after putting so many long hours getting ready. Even after our trucks and equipment were loaded and on their way, we had to pack and store everything we weren't taking with us. We won't be coming back to the same buildings or motorpool we are in now, or I should say, were in. One day in the motorpool, everyone laid out what they were going to store and we traded items. It was like a huge garage sale and highly against the regs!

One night, I came home with the worst headache I have ever had. I felt so bad because it was one of the few times Jason and I were together. He was so good to me and put me in the tub and ran cool water over my temples until the pain eased and I could sleep. Sleep, what a precious commodity.

We both agree we hate wasting what could be our last moments together for a long time by sleeping, but we just can't keep our eyes open. Once while we were asleep, someone walked by and said, "You'd think those two were married!" I had my head on Jason's shoulder. Sergeant W was sitting across from us and told them, "They are!"

I am glad Jason is here with me. I am trying to savor every moment that we can stay awake anyway. It is so hard to keep from touching him and showing the affection that flows so naturally between us, but we are in uniform and that would be fraternizing. I guess we were trying to be sneaky holding hands underneath the Pan-Am blanket, but I am so scared. Scared of war, scared of being separated, scared of all the unknown. I was just getting used to sharing my life with someone and I have no idea when he will be removed from my life.

I hope you won't have any trouble canceling our reservation for our wedding reception. Certainly when we put the deposit down, we could never have guessed all this would happen! I am certainly disappointed that we won't have the chance to have our church wedding. Well, perhaps someday we will.

Wish I could pretend that we have put the honeymoon before the church wedding. We flew over the Alps, and I thought of all the skiing I could do there. One of our refueling points was Rome, Italy. I was glued to the window of the plane, because I wanted to see Rome so bad. I couldn't see a single thing because fog lay low and thick, and I'm surprised the plane was even allowed to land. I think I might have seen St. Peter's Basilica, but I'm not sure. It might just have been my imagination conjuring up an image in the haze. We also stopped at Bangor, Maine. Poor Al, a guy from Jason's platoon is from Bangor. We couldn't get off the plane at either place, but then we were only there long enough to refuel the plane. Soon we will be touching down in Saudi Arabia and I just have no idea what to expect!

Love, Mary E.

October 10, 1990
Dear Dad,

When we first got here it was dark so I had no idea what it was like. Immediately after stepping off the plane, Jason and I were snagged for a detail. We were in a line handing off cargo. First we relayed boxes of water, and then we were off loading duffle bags. I tried to stick really close to Jason, because I never knew when we would be separated. But the detail ended and I lost him in the shuffle of bodies. I was told to get on this bus, one of several, and I have never had such a sinking feeling. I didn't know anyone on the bus. Just before it departed, one familiar face, a sergeant I had seen before, maybe in the motor pool, took the seat next to me. I still felt like I was being plunged into an abyss of unknown.

We arrived at what we now know as "Tent City." As I filed off the bus, my Sergeant T was there assisting with bag retrieval and told me where to find our section. Mercifully, the tents were already set up and it was about 3:00am when I collapsed onto a cot, more mentally exhausted than physically tired. I managed a little sleep before 6:00am wake-up.

I saw Jason's duffle bags last night when trying to find mine, so I figured our chances of meeting up again were good. Sergeant T ducked his head into the tent this morning and said, "Your husband is two tents down." It took all the military bearing I had to suppress the urge to run down and see for myself. The females have been told that we shouldn't go anywhere with out an "escort." Jason came to find me later and we went to breakfast. It is nice to have my built-in escort.

It sounds like we are basically in a holding pattern until our vehicles arrive. Word is my section will be informally attached to the 1st Cavalry Division Main (D-Main.) Word is Jason's section will go support the Tiger Brigade of the 2nd Armored Division. I hate to sound like a clique, but only time will tell.

Love, Mary E.

October 14, 1990
Dear Mom,

I can sum this place up in one word, HOT! Not that I can tell you why, but we borrowed a vehicle to go a different area today, so I got to see a little more than rows upon rows of canvas in Tent City. Basically, I saw sand, sand, and more sand everywhere. I find it interesting how many road signs are in English and Arabic. The Arabic writing looks pretty, but I'm sure it is hard to learn. It's almost hard to imagine it is really a language. As soon as I use up my laundry soap, I will send the box to you so you can see Tide written in Arabic. I would send you a can of Pepsi, but I'm not sure how that would travel.

Today was the first day we strayed from our usual schedule. Right now a typical day starts with reveille. Then we have PT (physical training), break, breakfast, training, lunch, training, supper, details and finally some personal time. Jason's platoon has been wearing their protective masks for 3-4 hours a day as a sort of endurance training.

I think my endurance training is to brave a shower. They are very cold. You would think in all this heat the water would warm naturally, but they are snatch-your-breath-away cold. That doesn't bother me half as much as some of the disgusting behavior taking place. Ever since a pit viper bit a soldier in the latrine, some people have been defecating in the shower! Gross! The soldier was rushed to the hospital ship, Mercy, which we can see over in the harbor. I heard a rumor that he lost his foot and a kidney, but that is pure rumor. I really don't know what happened. I do know it hasn't taken me long to remember to check for "Jake the Snake" in the latrines and shake out your boots in the morning.

The food is, well, not like home. Everything is canned. We get a Pepsi with our lunch, and when we are really lucky, we get a semi-cool one at supper. I really wish I could have a gallon of milk. We get just one little pint a day at breakfast. Apparently my milk withdrawal isn't as bad as the people who are having trouble with a lack of alcohol. There have been some soldiers trying to raid the Red Cross care packages for Scope or Listerine, or trying to buy cough syrup from anyone who had brought some along with them. It is going to be a long haul for some folks.

Do you remember the episodes of M*A*S*H when it is so hot? That is kind of like it is here in the evenings during our personal time. We sit and try not to be hot, which is impossible. It's nice to try and get out of the tents. Yesterday, Jason and I walked up to the edge of the harbor. A guy was throwing some bread in the water and sand sharks came right up and ate it! It was very intriguing to watch! The sharks made the water swirl and surge, but you couldn't see them until they came up out of blue-green water to grab the bread. Those poor sharks may regret eating Army food. I know there are times when I do, but beggars can't be choosers. That goes for the sharks too.

Love, Mary E.

October 16, 1990
Dear Dad,

We've been in a flurry of activity since our vehicles have arrived. We have a makeshift motor pool that we now go to at least once a day to check and double check on our vehicles. I presume we will be on the move soon, but even if did know, well, I couldn't tell you.

I had quite a bit of work to do on my poor old truck when it got here. Apparently there had been a fire on board ship and my truck was covered with soot. Someone said another vehicle had been struck by lightning, started burning and was then pushed overboard. All I know, I was stuck in the motor pool trying to wash soot off my truck with a rag and a very limited amount of bottled water. I did it because I was ordered to, but I certainly didn't make much progress with the task.

On my way back from the motor pool, I couldn't believe my eyes. I ran into Randy from Fredericksburg! I didn't even know he was in the Army let alone right here in Tent City. He has since pulled out, but it was nice to see a home familiar face even for a couple of minutes. How bizarre to run into a former high school classmate in

Saudi Arabia! Maybe you should let his folks know I saw him and he looked well.
Love, Mary E.

October 21, 1990
Dear Mom,

Jason is gone. I knew it was coming and I am so thankful of the extra moments I have had with him. Wives at home have been without their husbands longer than I have. I even gained one more day than I thought.

Two nights ago, I walked Jason to the edge of Tent City. He was going up to the motor pool to leave. I couldn't follow him all the way up there because I wouldn't have anyone to walk me back. I probably would have gone, but Jason said, "No, this is far enough."

If it had been during the day, that might have been one thing, but in the dark of night, no way. We walked in silence, as if talking in these last moments would break some sort of spell and we would be instantly separated. In the shadow of the gate, I risked fraternization and kissed him goodbye. Fighting the urge to cling to him, our hands remained tightly locked until he was too far out of reach.

I watched him trudge out the gate and up the steep embankment to the motor pool. I stood transfixed until I couldn't see him anymore, part of me wanted him to turn around one last time, the other part of me thought if he did, I would have run after him like a foolish school girl.

It's hard, Mom. I know I am a United States Army soldier. Where is my decorum, my discipline? All I could think of was I don't have any idea when I will see him again, and the heartache was stronger than the soldier and I went to the latrine and bawled. I didn't dare go back to my tent until I had myself under control. Trying to hide my red and swollen eyes, I went to bed, although I didn't get very much sleep. All night my ears were straining to hear the convoys leaving the motor pool. I kept thinking, "Is that him leaving?" "Is that his convoy?"

I got up following the same general routine, and when it came time for breakfast, I couldn't believe my eyes! Jason was there to escort me. It took all my will power not to run and jump into his arms in my excitement for this unexpected surprise. They had been delayed a day.

So, last night was similar to the night before, but I seemed more light-hearted. We chitchatted as we walked, admonishing each other to stay safe, to not get sick, to eat well. After I risked another kiss, he pinched my cheeks and said, "I love you, remember that!" I smiled and replied, "I love you, too!" He turned and was gone up and over the hill. This night the ache in my chest was more like having to say good night when we were dating. The "oh, I will miss you, but see you tomorrow" feeling, not the deep-seated agony of separation from the night before. I kept thinking, he'll be back again, but this morning I had no escort to breakfast. He is not here. I can feel the despair welling under the surface of the soldier. Mom, I don't know how I am going cope with this. Physical endurance of hardships is one thing, but this mental anguish! I'm not so confident on this front.
Love, Mary E.

October 21, 1990
Dear Jason,
        I'm waiting here desperately hoping I get to see you one more time. Maybe if I was on the move, I would have something to occupy my mind, but I don't know if we are going or not. It changes every hour it seems. I don't know if going with Division is good or bad either. One of the few things I do know is either way there will be details and more details. Lift this water box, do KP, fill that sandbag, fun and more fun.
        Well, I just saw them take down your tent. Guess that's pretty final. See you in the spring, huh? I guess the basic gist of this letter is to tell you just how much I love you. I promise, I will be good while we are apart. I'll go to sick call if I need to, eat MREs if I have to and be as safe as I can as long as you do to too, because we have to come back to each other in top form. Can't wait for that day!
Love, Mary E.

October 22, 1990
Dear Jason,
        Greetings from Fort Carson, Colorado – OH, was I dreaming out loud? You left your drive-on rag here. What will you wear over your face now? Don't inhale too much dust! I put it in a plastic bag so that it will smell like you longer. Do you suppose there is something strange about sleeping curled up with a plastic bag?

I named my M-16 today, Prudential. You know, the life insurance? He says he will take care of me until you can do it yourself. Let me tell you though, it sure a lot harder to "spoon" an M-16!

It sure seems weird around here without you. OH! I almost forgot to tell you that your old Lieutenant stopped by to talk with us this morning. He sure misses you guys by the way he talks. He hates his new assignment and he leaves tonight for the interior. He told me not to worry because you guys are the best. It made me feel good that someone else agrees with my assessment of you.

Today is the most humid yet. Just sitting here writing I'm sweating. We are still in green BDUs so I had to dig in my bags and it's a winter material – hot! I've got so much laundry to do, but not enough time before formation and now they say we might move today. I'm ready to move out.

I heard yet another rumor that if we don't move out, we might move to a warehouse. I hope not. I would just as soon keep my sand floor over being cooking in a tin can! I had to grab an MRE for later today. It is gross beef stew. I'll put the peaches in the envelope along with this letter Hope they find you too. I'm sorry, a person just can't be raised on Iowa corn-fed beef and then successfully eat whatever it is they are passing off as beef in the beef stew! At least there was cherry kool-aid inside.

Well, I'm off to cot detail. I'm sure glad all those people took the time to put those cots away right so I don't have to take practically everyone apart to do it right. Yes, I am being very sarcastic. At least I will get a break to go to church this morning.
Love, Mary E.

October 23, 1990
Dear Jason.

Hey, your old Lieutenant was in church yesterday! Then he stopped by again last night. Boy, he sure is lonely for you too. I'm pretty sure in a different way!

I wore my drive-on rag to PT this morning only on my head instead of across my face, as the sweat keeps dripping in my eyes. They were teasing me about it and were calling me Sister Mary Mary! I have even less time this morning than usual as I am on detail this morning. (Yeah, I know, what a shock!) It is tent detail. They off-loaded an awful lot of tents yesterday while I was on cot detail. It's going to be a long morning.

Back again. Eight of us moved twenty-five tents! Just about all the GP medium tents are gone, but all those larges are still there. As soon as we got back, we had to pack. We are leaving at sunrise. OH! There was a mouse in our tent! George and I chased it to get a better look at a Saudi mouse, but he just ran too fast. I swear there were dolphins in the gulf this morning. No matter what they were, they were sure big out in the water!

It has been decided that I will ride instead of drive tomorrow. Just driving the truck in the motorpool, all the guys give me a second look. I hate to imagine if a Saudi would have seen me. I have no desire to do any jail time over here, especially for simply doing the required elements of my job! Have you heard if they have released those female MPs yet? It's ok with me; it'll give me a good chance to gawk anyway. Well, my lieutenant is saying last call for mail, so bye! Love, Mary E.

October 23, 1990
Dear Jason,

Yes, I know I wrote you once already today. I just wanted to let you know, in case they don't get to you, I have sent you two letters before this one. One had a white chocolate candy bar in it and the other the soap case you left behind. If you don't get them please know I tried. We are sleeping here in the motorpool tonight. Well, we are supposed to be sleeping, but we are right underneath the light and right by the gate where the trucks drive in and out. I guess I better get used to the noise. The generators for our decoys will have to run 24-7.

I love you very much and I will keep writing at every chance, but word is…well, I might not be able to in the near future so, don't think I'm forgetting. I'm sure you know what the deal is too! I sure do love you! I took a shower tonight. Who knows when I'll have that chance again.

We missed *Major Dad* on TV tonight, or would that be last night? No, it hasn't been on yet. Either way we didn't get to watch it. I miss little things like snuggling on the couch watching TV. The things we take for granted! Well, I better try and get some rest it is nearly midnight and we are supposed to roll at 4:30am.
Love, Mary E.

October 24, 1990
Dear Jason,

Convoys kept leaving all night so there wasn't any sleep to be had. The tanks were so loud! We were all up at 3:00am only to find out at 4:30am we weren't going to roll until 6:00am. It was a wild ride as we drove into the desert with our bodies stacked on top of our gear like living cordwood. We were being tossed about in the back of a two & ½ ton truck like the frantic bucks of a mustang being broke to ride.

Now that we are here in the middle of nowhere it's like the Division won't acknowledge we are with them. They aren't making life very easy for us. Sergeant W couldn't find anyone with any info, so we finally just put up our tents and tried to settle in as well as you we can settle out here. I put your picture up by making a shelf. I put a board between my two duffle bags. Sure wish we would have gone with you guys. I hope things aren't this 8-up for you. A couple of the male types went to scout out a store. Can you imagine? And they talk about women, but it's the guys that can't live without a store, well, more like can't live without the smokes.
Love, Mary E.

October 26, 1990
Dear Dad,

To think people spend money for exotic vacations, when all they need to do is come here. I've traveled to a new country; I'm camping out; I get to read and write; I'm losing weight and I'm getting paid for all of this magnificence! Some kind of deal! I'll try to describe life here. I live in a tent with three female sergeants. The tent is probably about twelve feet in diameter with no floor. The desert sand is our floor. I have a cot, a little piece of board about six inches wide and a foot long, to put my feet on. My furniture is an old water box for storing a few things. It's pretty cramped, but it's home.

The latrines are screened plywood outhouses with a seat leading to a collection barrel underneath. Not the most comfortable, but it beats a plain hole in the ground. The deluxe four holers are on the far end of the camp. It's a long walk, but at least we don't have to smell them in the hot Saudi sun. Still, it seems an especially long hike at night. Some fellas seem to overcome this distance by urinating into empty water bottles. It is highly frowned upon to pee outside the tent. What may seem like a good idea at night becomes a haven for the ever-present hordes of flies in the day, not to mention the shear "gross-ness." When our neighbors, the LRSD guys (Long Range Surveillance Detachment) pulled out, there was a ring of yellow filled water bottles where their tent had been. Yes, picking them up was another one of those most rewarding details I have been on.

But by far, the absolute worst detail to be on is human waste burning – Yuk! We have to collect the full cans from the latrines and replace them with empty ones. Then the full cans are taken to the trash point. There we add diesel fuel, stir it and then try to light it without blowing anything up. It makes an awful black smoke and the smell is nauseating. The whole duty is repulsive and by far my least favorite! I would prefer to have KP for a week straight than one day of poop! Talk about your toxic waste!

For showers, we have little wooden stalls. Three together with one water tank on top. I'm so short that I have to jump up to reach the "on" lever and then jump back up to push "off." We have wooden pallets underneath us and I just know one of these days I am going fall through the slats and break an ankle. I don't dare leave the water run, though. First, that would waste way too much precious water and second, the water is so cold it takes your breath away. You have to shut the water off just to catch your breath.

The team in charge of building showers had to put tarps all the way around them because guys used to sit on the hill in front of the showers, trying to sneak peeks at us. They also went around and painted the water tanks black in hopes of absorbing the suns heat, but they used glossy paint. So, the showers are as cold as ever. Some people are hesitant to shower, and you can sure tell who they are! One crapper detail and you'd be running to the showers – cold or not!

We do have laundry service at this place, but I only send uniforms and T-shirts. Females aren't allowed to send underwear, and apparently white underwear is especially taboo to the Saudis. White is all I have. So, I have a Tupperware bowl I brought from home and wash them out by hand and hang them to dry outside on the ropes of the tent. You have to choose your tent ropes wisely. Too close to the front and everyone walking by sees your underwear and too close to the back and my fellow male platoon members gaze at my glorious underwear from their tent. Not that it should really matter out here, but I suppose I would like to believe I can maintain some personal decorum.

You have to do your laundry early in the day so that it is dry and back inside before the afternoon sandstorm. I swear on most days you could set you watch by the sandstorm.

Other details have been guard duty, filling sand bags and KP. When we aren't on detail, we are training or reviewing procedures. Lately, I've had detail every day, mostly KP. It's not too bad. I get up around 4:30am and work until 9:00am or 10:00am and if there isn't any supper, that's it for the day and it's back to regular training.

We don't usually get supper, just one hot meal a day. The cooks don't really cook, they mostly heat up water and put in T-rations. "T" rats are canned everything, vacuum-sealed food in a tin about the size of a square cake pan; one meat, one starch, one veggie equals about twelve soldiers. So far, all we have had is beef and carrots in gravy, with rice and carrots on the side. It's not really all that bad, but of course people complain incessantly. I'm so meat-starved, I think it's great. Of course, it's not home. Heck, I'm not even sure it's real meat but it's warm and better than MREs.

I absolutely despise MREs – Meal made Ready to Eat. They come in a brown plastic pouch; everything inside is in vacuum-sealed pouches. The menus sound good, but they are really wretched! Chicken Ala King ingredients: chicken, water, chicken broth, chicken fat, modified food starch, mushrooms, peas, powdered vegetable shortening (partially hydrogenated soy oil, lactose, sodium caseinate, dipotassium phosphate, sodium silicoaluminate), dehydrated cream cheese (pasteurized milk and cream, nonfat dry milk, cheese culture, salt, carob bean gum, disodium phosphate), pimentos. Dehydrated onion, salt, dehydrated celery, dehydrated green peppers, lecitin, and spices – yummy!

Other tasty selections are: Beef, diced with gravy, Ham Slice, Chicken and Rice, Spaghetti and meatballs, and my all-time worst, Tuna and Noodles. Ironically, I try to get Tuna and Noodles, because they always have cheese and crackers inside and M & M's. Candy is like gold over here. In my opinion, MRE merits are based solely on what desert comes with it. The only things not scared of an MRE are the mean desert flies.

I usually trade my main dishes for cheese and crackers. My meals mostly consist of squishy pouch cheese and tasteless crackers with the consistency of hard tack. You don't dare forget to knead the cheese before opening it or you will get oily ooze followed by clumpy curds when you open the pouch.

I consider it to be my lucky day when I change from cheese and crackers to a rare peanut butter pouch with shelf-stable bread. Bread in a pouch, it looks like the miniature loaves we used to get at the state fair. The cooks toss out the bread to a frenzy of grabbing soldiers as if they were kids going after candy in a parade. I can only imagine how shelf-stable the bread is in my stomach. Ten years from now it will probably still be in my system!

People are very creative in heating their MREs. One popular method is putting the main course pouch on the manifold of a vehicle when driving from site to site. By the time you reach your destination your lunch is warm. I personally don't believe warming them up helps to choke them down!

The accessory packet contains a piece of gum, salt, pepper, Tabasco sauce, matches, a packet of coffee and an itty-bitty piece of toilet paper that barely serves as a Kleenex to blow your nose let alone its intended duty. Tabasco and coffee can be other hot commodities. I've heard that if you douse an MRE main course with enough Tabasco sauce, it doesn't matter how bad it is.

MREs make KP bearable. I try to remember that when I am elbow deep in a garbage can full of ice-cold oily wash water searching for utensils hidden in the silt on the bottom of the can. The system to trying to wash pots and dishes in the desert is a series of three garbage cans filled with water. Wash, rinse, and rinse. Of course this is the desert so we only change the water once every three days. That's what garbage can lids are made for.

They have submersible heaters that are supposed to heat the final rinse in efforts to sanitize, but it's give or take it if they will work or not. There is a definite technique to lighting them and I have yet to try it. They surely make for an odd picture with their long smoke stack protruding from a garbage can.

Now mind you, to dry the pots, dishes and pans, we lay them out on wooden pallets where a nice layer of sand covers them before we can get them put away. One day, the wind was in the wrong direction. The chimney of an actual working submersible was puffing away and sent a layer of residue all over the drying pots.

On the rare occasions that we are served a supper, I have washed the dishes in the dark. It didn't take me long to figure out the priority scale of dishes you really need to see to wash and those that can be washed by touch. What would we do without challenges?

I know it sounds like I am being pretty negative, Dad, but I do try and keep a positive out look and wear a smile on duty. I know you say that there is something good in everything, but I'm not sure right now what that good might be, it must be there somewhere!

On detail, people have made comments to me like, "You must be from the Midwest. You work too hard." One day, we had to pick up rocks on a hill to fill a drainage system ditch. It reminded me of picking up rocks out in the fields back on our farm or picking up hickory nuts with Grandma down in the woods. I wonder, has Grandma been out picking up hickory nuts this fall? Was there a good crop of them?

Everyone is so unhappy about being away from home, but it doesn't do any good to be sour. Working hard helps relieve that frustration and at least you are passing time. Still, I never get that feeling of satisfaction as I do working on the farm. I miss and love you so very much.

Love, Mary E.

October 26, 1990
Dear Jason,

First things first, I love you more than all the sand in this desert. Heck, all the desert sands everywhere. So, how is life at your desert resort? Are you going to be leaving there soon? I wanted to come to your site for a visit, but I had KP yesterday when the rest of the team went up to your site and of course they aren't going today. KP was hard work yesterday. Dave and I had to help them move, situate, off-load water, MREs and T-rations. Then, we had to load and dump the garbage and then, get this we had to destroy over 1,000 T-rations that we had just off-loaded! We had to punch holes in their lids. I was covered in various veggie juices all because of a major's order. Seems like such a waste, seems that the food could go to someone who could use it. Apparently, it was expired. I didn't know Army food could expire.

I heard the Major wants to make things like garrison over here. Dress right bunks and boots under the bed and polished at that. Seems pretty unrealistic to me.

Gotten any mail? None for me. You have written, haven't you? By the way, D-Main finally recognized we are with them, so note the new address again! Mine takes up so much space there is hardly enough room for your address, which takes up plenty of space itself!

I see people around every so often; wish it was you I was running into. I see Ron from your platoon every now and then when he is over here driving your Major. Our Fred is still driving bus. One day I even saw him driving a double decker.

Love, Mary E.

October 27, 1990

Dear Jason,

Sure do love you! I'm really mad! My truck goes to your site at least two times a day now and I'm not allowed to go. I don't even know if you're there or not. I got cancelled off the latest mission, so I'm going to get detailed to death. As if I'm not now, but there will be even less of us enlisted peons to do the bidding of the masters.

Last night, I was supposed to be on bunker building detail and only two of us showed up. The other private happened to be in the Division Chief of Staff office. She confirmed the rumor we heard about not wearing our floppy hats because the General doesn't think he looks good in it! She said we'd be able to wear it on R&R. She also said the Army has ordered us swimsuits because there will be a pool at the R&R place. R&R, hmm… what do you suppose the likelihood of that happening would be? Yeah, I didn't think so either.

Seen any nasty animals yet? Knock on wood, I haven't yet. The secretary said she saw nearly a dozen scorps yesterday all under sandbags, so be careful. Please, please be careful. I love and miss you so much!

Love, Mary E.

October 28, 1990

Dear Jason,

I sure enjoyed seeing you today! What a nice surprise too! I couldn't believe I got leave this site, let alone be given permission to visit you. My mind was racing on the drive back because I couldn't cry in front of Sergeant E, but I just hated leaving you. I sure enjoyed our brief moment together, but leaving was so hard.

Poopy report You must really be good for my body and soul. I finally had to go after I got back from seeing you. Well, it was you or the MRE bread, ha! Pretty scary when poop becomes newsworthy! We got some ice today and while Sergeant T unpacked the light set he had acquired during the motorpool garage sale. So, I'm sitting on my cot drinking ice water and writing without the use of a flashlight. Talk about the lap of luxury. The guys even dug a pit for the generator so it doesn't even sound that loud. We have to keep the tent flaps down though for light discipline. It can make it stuffy in here! Double edged sword, huh? I feel a little guilty knowing you won't have any generators. I hope you will be extra careful with your candles, especially when playing spades! One wrong move and your tent would go up faster than I hate to imagine! I know that candles are cheaper and easier to come by than flashlight batteries, but…be careful!

Ok, questions I wanted to ask you, but just didn't have enough time: Do people own the desert? And if they do, do they look at it and love like we love Iowa and Oregon? We think that our homes are so beautiful, but as I survey this land, I just see a barren, ugly, hurtful land. What do you think?

Well, I've got to go now. I'm sure glad I was able to steal a kiss from you today! It will go far!
Love, Mary E.

October 29, 1990
Dear Jason,

I hate to imagine what your area must be like today. We are having an all day dust storm. We can't even see from one end of camp to the other. We had a class today to refresh us on M-60 machine gun loading, clearing, disassemble and assemble. It was ok. I don't know why it is so important to know if they aren't going to let us have any ammo for the thing anyway. Guard duty sure caught up with me because I'm extra tired. Everyone seems so fond of giving orders around here so these are mine for you. Eat four meals a day – no skipping and drink lots of water and rest as much as you can for now because I need you and I love you very much.
Love, Mary E.

October 30, 1990
Dear Jason,

OK bitch-fest – you have been warned. Sergeant E has a huge case of the ass – what a jerk. He's going to turn this into one big picnic – what an ass – I can't think of big enough words to call that prick. Do this PFC, do that – I got fed up and plain told him No! I know that's disobeying an order. I'll fill you in later!!

OK, I'm back and only ten hours later! I've got just a few moments of free time to finish this letter. The story is as follows: The guys put a shower they brought from home, another Sergeant T trade, right behind their tent and their tent is behind ours so I had to help dig a pit around it so it wouldn't run into the tents. Plus we had to gather rocks to put in there. I had the impression this was a platoon project. Then Sergeant E said females would not be able to use it. I asked why the four of us (well actually three since Sergeant V never seems to take showers which is a whole other story) were exempt. He informed me that is was their personal shower. So I said, "Fine, I'm done helping then." Sergeant E said, "PFC, pick up the shovel and fill sandbags!" I replied, "No, I'll pitch in and help all you want for the platoon, but don't tell me to do your personal projects just because I'm a PFC." Sergeant E was just fuming mad, and I did help to finish. I didn't want to give him any fuel for not letting me go see you again or be accused of not following orders, but I did take up the issue with Sergeant W. She agreed with me.

With our site pretty well set up, we started training too. We broke out the computers and the night vision goggles and went over some tactics. I sure didn't mind all of the activity. I think it was the quickest day I have spent over here. I have KP tomorrow. About half of us are leaving soon on a mission. I'll be left here so, I'm probably going to be dogged even worse. Some of the guys said they saw you today on a water run. I'm jealous. I assume Sergeant E will never let me out of this camp again, so I'm afraid I'll never get to see you.

This has been some dust storm, huh? We have had to use extra stakes and sand bags on our tent down and we have to tighten all the ropes about every hour. I hope you got your tent flaps down in time! Wonder what Halloween will be like? I'm sure no different than any other day. Hey, do you suppose Sergeant E would let me go trick or treating to your site?
Love, Mary E.

October 31, 1990
Dear Jason,

Happy Halloween! Well, we are going to tell ghost stories tonight in honor of the day. As of tonight, it has been 12 mail calls and not a single letter or stitch of mail from anyone! To be very

honest and only to you, I'm about ready to cry, but I would NEVER cry in front of these people. Why does everyone day after day get letters and packages too, but not me? I know you are writing because you told me so, but why don't I hear from anyone else? I know they MUST be trying, right? I have to admit, I feel so alone. It's so easy for people to tease too, because they hear from home. Sergeant R called my name like I finally had a letter and as I got up he said, "You didn't get anything, again." Why are people so mean? I am writing furiously, because, I will not, I WILL NOT cry, but I can't stand this. I know I am being a total wimp, but is it so unreasonable to want one letter? I keep writing and writing and I don't know if any of these letters are making it to anyone. Sergeant K's husband writes her "in country" and his letters get here in three days. Three days! I'm sorry this letter is sad, but I am a sad person and all I can do is write that fact down on paper. I will not allow myself to show such weakness to these people. I know that I'm not really alone and that I carry you, God and my family with me in my heart. I know too that God has blessed me with you, but some how that still doesn't prevent me from really, really wanting a big hug when I feel blue. I love you! I am imagining your strong arms around me so don't worry. I'll be ok and thanks for listening.
Love, Mary E.

November 1,1990
Dear Jason,
       You'll never believe this, but someone stole my bayonet while I was on KP this morning. Our weapons are supposed to be secured? The Major threatened to search the tents if it wasn't returned and someone slipped it under the tent! Swish!
       I have been requested to be a chaplain's assistant, but I'm sure it will not be approved. My detail expertise is indispensable. It would sure be nice to get some mail today. Hope you are getting mail as well as the goodies I try to send on to you.
Love, Mary E.

November 2, 1990
Dear Jason,
       I have been reading a lot lately on our down times or load times. I hate to sit around. I found a copy of <u>Gone With the Wind</u>. That should last me a little while. It means so much more to me now

especially being separated from the man that I love! I just read the part where Melanie and Ashley go to their room leaving Scarlett alone. I was just thinking what I would do if I was Melanie and you were Ashley. I would hug the stuffing out of you first of all. The first time I read this book it seemed glamorous, but now I seem to gain insight to the realities of war. Although I am not directly fighting for life as I know it, I can somehow identify with Ashley. I agree that wars are bad and bring nothing but misery. I don't want to be here. I definitely don't thrive on hardships; yet, I do feel that I'm obligated to be here because it is my patriotic duty to be where I am needed. I just keep wishing life was happy again. Just like Ashley's wish for the return of his way of life. They could never go back and I don't want to either, but I do want to be together. I'm sure you have no idea what I'm writing about so I'll stop for now. I just miss you so much and I want to be with you like a wife and husband should be. We should be talking about our futures and our life together, not wondering how the other is and if some crazy man is going to take our lives away. I love you.

Later: Well, I've got guard duty tonight. I guess there have been wild dogs around. Sure hope that is only a rumor. The thought of wild dogs roaming and preying in the dark almost scares me more than the humans.

I tried to get some sleep this afternoon when I found out I had guard duty, but I didn't succeed. It's Friday night. Everyone else we know is probably rejoicing at the prospect of a weekend. We are stuck in this…place. Well, I guess I should clean Prudential again. I want him to work right if we are over run. If it weren't for the fact that everyday is one closer to you (I think) I'm not sure I could get up in the morning for you are my sunshine and my starlight. I'll make lots of wishes on the falling stars and I'll see you in my daydreams.
Love, Mary E.

November 2, 1990 (written on Chicken Ala King MRE box)
Dear Mom, Grandma & Grandpa,

HI! Well, I haven't gotten any mail yet! Except the October church letter two days before the supper! I saw I was mentioned but they forgot Jason! You guys haven't forgotten about him, have you? Please, please don't! Since mail takes so long I'll ask now-for Christmas can you please send Jason a box of white chocolate candy bars? He loves white chocolate. I hope you still have his address. It

hasn't changed. You don't have to send me anything-just Jason. Sure love you guys and miss you too!
Love, Mary E.

November 2, 1990
Dear Mom,

I kind of wanted to share with you some thoughts that a girl shares with her Mom. Mom, I am tired of being your tumultuous daughter. Doesn't it seem that everything I get involved with always has something added to it? Always an extra wall to climb, or obstacle to overcome. I admit it's partly my fault, but this time, I had no say. I hate this place! Is God punishing me for not liking Texas by sending me to a place 100 times worse? Have I been *that* bad in my life? I'm tired of eating food out of a box that is covered with sand by the time it goes from the box to your mouth! I'm tired of using a latrine that you have to clean before you use it and not wanting to take the time to poop for fear of flies landing on your privates! I'm tired of sweating all day and freezing all night. I'm tired of outside showers with freezing water and men sitting in the hills with binoculars trying to catch peak at your boobs when you turn your water on and off. Heck, I'm tired of showers you can't leave run for fear of running out of water. I'm tired of checking everything for scorpions! I'm tired of never getting mail – none! I'm tired of digging sand bags and burning human waste and working hard so someone else can take a break! Most of all, I'm tired of being away from my husband and although I write him practically every day, we don't get mail!

I'm tired of men and women with loud swearing, filthy mouths and, Mom, I'm tired of washing clothes by hand only to have dust blow on them while they dry. I'm tired, tired, tired and there's not a darn thing I can do! I'm just plain tired of being dirty and alone. Oh, I know, we are never really alone. God is with us and so is the love of Jason and all of you, but Mom I just want to cry. I have so long to go before I can come home. I hate the thought of being away from everyone for Thanksgiving, Christmas, my birthday, and for a girl to have to cancel her own wedding! Yes, Mom, I know and I really am trying to be grateful for the things we do have! I know Uncle Jim had to go through this and a whole lot worse in World War II. I don't want war, but we know it is coming. The waiting and the unanswered questions are awful. All the wishing and praying in the world can't make this end tonight. All I want, Mom, is to be happy.

I've had a glimpse at my happiness, but it seems to have been stripped away by a madman.

Mom, I'm sorry to unload all of this on you. I know I am pitifully whining. I try to give Grandma and Grandpa good reports of what goes on here. I surely don't want them to worry. I don't really want to worry you either. I probably shouldn't even send this letter. I sure could use one of your bone crunching hugs! I sure love and miss you so much. Well, I have to get ready for guard duty. Last time there were so many falling stars to wish on.
Love, Mary E.

November 3, 1990
Dear Jason
Had guard duty last night and it's taking all the energy I can muster to get up and write to you. D-main duty roster came out and I was to have guard again tonight, but Sergeant W said I shouldn't get stuck with it practically every night so I am now on KP. I'm not terribly fond of KP, but it is better than twelve grueling hours of nothingness. Everyone is getting ready to go to the PX at D-rear, but I'm staying here. Hopefully everyone will go. They are all saying they want to go and get away from here, but to be quite honest I want to be away from all of them. Privacy and personal time are so rare. My only escape seems to be my Walkman and writing letters. I hope you are getting the things I am sending to you along with my letters. Hope you got your soap holder, the white chocolate bars and the MRE parts I don't use. Although the moon has been up all night lately during guard duty, I keep wishing on falling stars I do see for you. I guess the one good thing about guard duty is when you finally get to sleep you are so tired you don't dream.

I had a nightmare the other night. There were muddy flood waters everywhere. We were in two boats but it was like they were moving as one as we were being whisked along by the flood. We looked up into hills and water was running like fast muddy creeks but it was all going across the hills instead of down. Then, the water started splitting us apart and as the torrent kept taking us farther and farther apart the water on the hills started running up hill. Then, your boat just stopped, while I kept moving faster and faster until I could no longer see you or even any land. It seemed like I was in Noah's flood only all alone in a rickety old boat in the middle of swirling muddy water. Hmm…perhaps guard duty isn't so bad after all.

Love, Mary E.

November 4, 1990
Dear Jason,
      Well, I received a letter from you today! I was so happy! So, you will be leaving on a mission? Half of me wants you to go because I'm sure you want to do you job and I want you to do your job too, but I don't want you to go into any danger, as if there is a place like that around here! The two wants just don't seem to match up do they? Gotta go...
      Well, I had to pick up and move as the Lieutenant came in and wanted to talk about promotions. I turned to Sergeant V knowing that it was my cue to excuse myself from the AO and said, "Well, this is one conversation I have to stay out of." LT turned and just reamed on me saying, "Private, you know I have no control over promotions and if you keep that attitude I'll stop any promotions for you." Did that make any sense to you? It didn't make any to me either. First, he has no control and second he does? And me just trying to politely exit the tent. Man, what a pissy mood. I'm getting a little tired of all this attitude being let out on us lower enlisted. Talk about things rolling down hill! I guess I'll just have to keep my mouth totally shut. Privates apparently are on the same level as children. You are to be seen and preferably working, but definitely not heard! And they say we complain all the time? Funny how one minute the Division First Sergeant and a Major are giving me a compliment and the next minute I am in the doghouse with an LT and my own sergeant. Earlier, I thought Sergeant W was asking my opinion on something and she just bit my head off! She was rearranging the teams and was apparently working the numbers out in her head. I simply stated, "I think more people should be on the physical team." She growled at me and said, "I know my job and I'll put people where I want them!"
      I know this will shock you, but I had KP again this morning. I have had KP so many times that the cooks look to me to assign duties to the other KPs. One other private told me this morning that he likes it when I am on KP because we get out of there an hour earlier than other times he's had it. Yes, I know it has nothing to do with my efficiency. I am just an inept private that allows shoddy work, right? Depends on who you ask apparently. Am I whining–again?
      So, will you be leaving soon on your mission? As if you could tell me. Please be careful when you do go. Does it mean that

our Bat-D is working if Hussein thinks we are on the verge of attack? Of course we might be and not even know it! I do want this to be over, but at what cost? If we do fight I'm afraid of the high amount of casualties. Please, please be careful and don't be one! Yesterday there was a low flying jet. It was so low and fast I didn't have a chance to identify. Did it pass over you too? Makes me a little jumpy but I guess that has to do with another dream I had. I dreamt that airplanes, jets and helicopters kept flying over us in huge numbers. The whole sky was full of them almost wing tip to wing tip. They just kept coming and coming almost like in the fall when the black birds start flying and they are so thick and all you can see from horizon to horizon is black birds yet they just keep coming and coming. Although, perhaps being in a city you know nothing of black birds migrating. Well, lets just say the dream was unnerving. Where are they coming from? Where are they going? What does it all mean? See? I need to go back to having guard duty so I can have mindless sleep the day after.

I do know I sure love you. I miss you so much it makes my chest ache and I can't do a thing but write to you and stare at your picture.

Love, Mary E.

November 5, 1990
Dear Mom,

Please disregard the last letter I wrote to you. I was just so homesick. Things aren't that bad. Still no mail from home, but I know you are writing. Please ask Grandma to send a box full of meatloaf, scalloped potatoes, creamed beans and that great chocolate cake with maple frosting. Of course, by the time it got here, it would probably make an MRE look tasty!

Love, Mary E.

November 5, 1990
Dear Jason,

I just received a letter from you. What a joy it is to hear from you! I wouldn't care (much) if I never got a letter from the States as long as I keep getting letters from you! Well, I must close for now. It is past 8:00pm and I have KP in the morning. This will be the third day in a row. I guess it is better than crap burning! Thank you for your letter. I love you so much.

Love, Mary E.

November 9, 1990
Dear Jason,

I HATE burn detail. It was the WORST! I'd gladly do KP instead of that! YUK! Oh! Dread, Yuk, Yuk, and Yuk! Well, I really don't have much to say today. It is nice and quiet around here as most everyone is gone. Seems almost strange to be here alone. Trying to get caught up on some letter writing to my folks. I hope you don't mind such short letters, but there is just so much I can tell you about the same old details.
Love, Mary E.

November 9, 1990
Dear Grandma,

Enclosed is a Saudi dollar. It's worth about 33 ½ cents to our dollar. Don't spend it in one place, now! Thanks so much for you letter! I was so happy to finally receive some mail! I wish I could have gone to the church supper with you. They are always so good.

Were you able to find a good sweater when you went shopping? I wish I had known early that you were looking for one. I sent most of mine to Susan because I sure don't need them here. Of course, they probably would have been way too big for you.

When I get home, will you teach me how to cook something other than frozen pizza and macaroni and cheese? I don't like pumpkin pie, but I sure would like to be able to make one for Jason along with turkey and stuffing, the Thanksgiving works! The sergeants in my tent are always talking about cooking and I'm listening, but I don't think anything beats practical hands on experience!

One day we had to pick up rocks off a hill to fill a drainage system. It reminded me of picking up hickory nuts with you. How funny it was to me that you should mention doing just that!

I wish I was as fortunate as Bev's son to have a barracks. Jason and I are out in the middle of the desert in tents. We are about fifteen miles apart, but it is far enough that is takes about two weeks for our mail to get to one another. I've seen him twice. We are very busy.

I miss him and all of you so very much. Once again, Grandma, thank you so much for writing to me. It is so nice to hear of home.

Love, Mary E.

November 10, 1990
Dear Jason,

Well, it seem that our LTs have a deal – yours tries to give us a little privacy and tries to get us together and mine seems determined to keep us apart. I wish I could have stopped by today because I was up your way. Got to follow those orders – Snap! Snap! I sure miss you. I'm sorry you've had bad dreams too, but I am glad you have had a chance to sleep. It seems rest should be a haven from this sandy existence, but when your sleep is invaded by goblins it is hard to know which is lesser of two evils.

I don't seem to find very many kindred spirits around here lately. I have had KP with one girl that I have tried to become friends with, but I find it hard at times to keep my patience. Jody is a bigger woman than me, but still finds it hard to lift even a water box! This of course puts her in the "woman working class category," which naturally makes me cringe. It also makes her rather inept at every detail we are assigned to. I've had to rewash many things that got too heavy and she dropped in the sand. I'm not sure how she ever got here in the first place. She seems very dependent without any opinions of her own. She seems frightened of everything including her job on KP and she's never sure of anything. I sometimes feel like I am babysitting and that seems tiring on top of all my own responsibilities.

This morning I had it with a cook. She was so growlly and disrespectful. I found it very hard to work for her. I told her "Look here, I am not you hand servant!" She is just a Spec4, one rank above me, but with that attitude you'd think she were a General (or worse yet a Lieutenant!) She went to her Sergeant to tell her what I had said, but she didn't make it too far down that road. Her Sergeant scolded her for being in such a bad mood. Her Sergeant knows I'm hard working and that I don't shirk my responsibilities.

The cook came back at me madder than ever and told me I have a bad attitude. I just laughed at her and said, "Well, that's certainly the pot calling the kettle black!" and turned and laughed all the way back to the wash bucket. I had to leave at 10:00am no matter

what as I had my own Bat-D duties to do, but we, thanks to slow
Jody, hadn't finished all the dishes, while the cook had gone back to
her tent to "rest." Stammering Jody was afraid to leave so I told her to
stay if she wanted but I HAD to go. I went to the cook laid out on her
cot and told her, "We're leaving." The cook replied, "I haven't
dismissed you!" I told her "That's all right, you don't have to, we are
leaving." I wish that cook would learn sugar catches more flies than
vinegar! Oh well, sure glad I signed up for the elite corps of Military
Intelligence-Ha!
Love, Mary E.

November 11, 1990
Dear Jason,
        I wrote a letter to you yesterday, but didn't send it because I
thought I was coming to see you. Somebody borrowed our truck and
so I couldn't come–bummer. Plus, I had KP again this morning. This
was supposed to be a detail free day. I have a box of stuff for you
filled with books and MRE parts. I finished *Gone With the Wind,* I put
that in your box too. I know you won't read it, but somebody up your
way may need it. You know, all the money in the world could never
make me happier than you do. I wouldn't care if I had to live my life
dirt poor as long as I had you! I love you.
Love, Mary E.

November 12, 1990
Dear Jason,
        Nothing of importance going on. I miss you terribly. I talked
to the Chaplain yesterday because I went to late church and for about
fifteen minutes I was the only one there. He's very nice and he prayed
for us by name. I thought that was nice. So, now he calls me Mare
whenever he sees me and he's a Lieutenant Colonel! I bumped
elbows, so to speak, with General T yesterday while I was on trash
detail. He looks just like my Uncle Dick!
        Had KP again this morning, but thank goodness we don't
have supper tonight. This morning on KP a Major stopped and said,
"I really appreciate your smile and cheer in the mornings. It makes
this place a bit more tolerable." Yes, can you believe it? After all the
whining I seem to do in your letters, it must be hard for you to
imagine me doing anything, but complaining. The best part for me
was that the Major is the one directly over my LT! I swear this place

has more Captains and Majors than PFCs and Spec4s. Maybe the Captains can start pitching in on details too, ha! What a sight that would be!

I still haven't heard from my mom, but at least I heard from Grandma and I got two nice letters from your dad. Did you remember I brought my University of Iowa correspondence class with me? I also received one of my homework assignments. I got an A. My professor said he admired me for continuing my class in such conditions. I find it interesting to be taking a Biblical Archaeology class so near to the locations in the class. So close and yet so far, huh? Kind how it is for us, isn't it? I love you so much!

Love, Mary E.

November 17, 1990
Dear Mom,

Hurrah! I finally got a letter from you! Boy was it ever nice! I am so glad to hear of the town's support. It makes me feel appreciated. I guess we have really been in the same waiting boat. I really am writing, Mom! See? It's hard waiting on both ends, isn't it? I'm just so thrilled to hear from you, I think I'm going to go and read your letter again. Thanks for making my day, Mom! I love and miss you heap-o-las!

Love, Mary E.

November 17, 1990
Dear Dad,

Greetings from your personal 1st Kevlar troop! Want an explanation? Our 1st Cavalry Division has been nicknamed 1st Kevlar because we have to wear our kevlars (steel pot, i.e. helmet) instead of the floppy desert hat. The reason? Good question, I have heard it is because the General doesn't think he looks good in the floppy hat! I don't know, but that's what I've been told. Finally, last week the General must have broken down because we can wear the floppy hat when we are "off-duty." Funny, it doesn't seem like we are ever off duty. It's not as if we can run home for the weekend or something!

The other day on KP, I was hauling some trash to the trash point; I looked up and saw this guy with a star on his collar. I thought to myself, who is that guy with a star? What country has stars on their uniform? Then as this "man" was coming toward me, it hit me–oh my! Duh! He's General T! He looks just like your brother! He asked me a few superfluous questions about being on duty, I certainly can't quote him. Before I even had time to answer, he walked away which was just as well. I can't believe I was so flustered, my word, he is just a man. Yet, I've never had a General speak to me before. Heck, I'm not sure I've even seen a General up close before.

Thanks to everyone for the letters and boxes. I appreciate it more than words can say. Honestly! The wet wipes are a hot commodity over here. They go for about $4.00 a dozen. I received some apple cider packets. That was great. I still don't drink coffee, and Saudi water, even bottled, leaves much to be desired. Just give me good ol' Iowa well water. What I wouldn't give to take a long drink from the pump in barn with the old tin cup.

Today is actually pleasant, not so hot. It has really been cooling down at night. That goes along with a definite increase in wind velocity. It's hard on my sinuses and everyone else's too. There isn't a morning I don't wake up with a sore throat. Cold showers don't help much either! I'm not complaining about weather. I'd rather freeze than melt off the face of the earth.

Darn flies!! They are MEAN!! Everything over here is mean. The more you swat them, the meaner they get. Scorpions are UGLY and mean. I've only seen pit vipers in the snake category and they certainly aren't friendly. Tangle with one of those and you are more likely than not to go home in a body bag! Dung beetles are persistent and annoying. I've heard camels are so mean they spit on you. I've only seen camels from afar. The closest was when I had to stop the truck while one crossed the road, VERY SLOWLY! Even plants are mean. Every plant seems to have a thorn or sticker on them. Some stickers get covered in the sand and when you get into it for sand bag detail they stick in your hands or go right through your clothes and into your knees–mean plant.

The weather is a lot drier here than at Tent City, and there is more room out here. Still, it doesn't really matter to me; everything has good and bad points about it. Sure, I get tired of washing clothes by hand and cold showers and open-barrel latrines, but it's better than nothing.

Tell that little sister of mine, Emily, to stop watching "Good Morning America." I'll never be on that show. NO ONE ever gets out this far. I guess we are intermediate front-line troops. We don't get nice things and important visitors like the rear troops. Still, we are not far enough up to get the "special" presents sent from companies for the front line troops. We are stuck at an unhappy medium. Isn't there a song about being stuck in the middle?

You asked if I was counting days, can't count them – we don't have a return date so there is nothing to count toward. We've heard everything from 1 Jan 91 to 1 Jan 92 and everything in between.

The winds are fairly calm right now. Everyday between noon and 2 o'clock a dust storm normally hits and sends us running, miserable, again. Please don't talk of snow and skiing. I have been hoping hard that Jason and I will return before the end of ski season. Enough said, except I've seriously considered slapping some boards on my boots and trying my hand a sand skiing! Wouldn't that be a sight?

Wow! That was low! Made me duck! A lot of air action today. Usually they are A-10s, but they are F-16s today. Can't really see, the wind has started to pick up. Time out to move inside my tent. Funny thing –if something did break out over here, my family would probably know before us just by watching CNN! Well, dust is starting to clog the pen. I'll take that as a sign to say good-bye. I miss you and love you all.

Love, Mary E.

November 18, 1990
Dear Dad,

Thanks for the letter. I feel compelled to answer tonight. I usually receive mail at night and read it and then try to answer in the morning. Tonight I will answer your letter first.

I have started receiving letters more frequently, but that doesn't mean you can stop! I have even received some letters from my new in-laws. They seem fairly enthusiastic about Iowans in the family. I guess David, my father-in-law has written to you too.

Please tell Ken that he is wrong about our location. Of course, I can't tell you where we are, but I can say we aren't there. I read the *Des Moines Register* article you sent and I was surprised to see them list a location. I was more surprised that someone would actually write it in a letter. That is such an OP SEC violation, but I guess that is just the MI in me. As for you, just keep guessing and eventually I'll be able to tell you where I have been.

I'm glad you had a good trip to Texas for the car. What did you think of Fort Hood? Grandma spilled the beans by telling me you actually liked the car. What? A two seater/two door? It's not BIG four-door Buick. Are you my dad? Just teasing!

As for the apartment inspection. I knew about the oven. I just didn't have the time to clean it before we left. Other than the oven, is your daughter a respectable housewife, even under pressure? It is such a relief to have it all taken care of. Thank you so much.

Hello again, sorry for the break, but I was off to another promotion ceremony. There are only two of us PFCs left and I am feeling a little impatient about getting my E-4 Specialist. I know learning patience is yet another character building experience. Seems everywhere I turn lately is a character building experience.

You asked me for suggestions on naming the new bull. Well, taking names from my surroundings I guess I would say how about helicopter names: Kiowa, Apache, Black Hawk, or Chinook? Wasn't there an Angus bull named Black Jack? Maybe I should suggest Spades, as that seems to be the card game of choice around here.

I do have some good news. I got an "A" in my U of Iowa class! Seems silly to keep plugging away at classes over here, but there will be life after Saudi. Besides, I have been taught to finish what I start! I can't believe how much I want to get back to school. I know I am not finished learning some lessons the hard way, but I am beginning to realize how important my education is now.

Well, I suppose I should get some sleep. I sure do miss and love you, Dad!
Love, Mary E.

November 19, 1990
Dear Jason,

Ok, I'm warning you right now. Don't even bother reading this letter, because I am whining. Sergeant W told me your hello message and that you stopped by here while I was on duty. It was all I could do to keep from crying-I was missing you terrible bad to begin with. Writing to you just doesn't seem to cut it. I want physical. I want to talk to you, look into your eyes. I think I could take any amount of BS thrown at me if only I wasn't separated from you. All I feel is this horrible and oppressive loneliness. I'm sick of relying on the faulty and slow mail system for brief bits of commentary. I don't know, I really don't know how I am going to make it through this whole thing. It hasn't really been that long and we have such a long time stretching out in front of us. Maybe in even years before we are

together again. I feel so helpless when the tomorrows seem to stretch out so far ahead. I try to be thankful for what we do have and what we have had together, but I would give up anything I have here to be with you. Someday, if we are ever together and I complain, remind me not to because I am with you. Well, I'm holding on for Thanksgiving and hopefully nothing bad will happen and we'll be able to spend it together. Well, at least an hour or two, which is better than none. Can't wait to feel your arms around me in one of those hugs I love so well!
Love, Mary E.

November 19, 1990
Dear Mom, Grandma and Grandpa,
 Thank you so much for the package! I certainly do appreciate it, every ounce of it! Grandma, you are without a doubt the world's greatest cookie maker! The kool-aid was wonderful, but the best all was the popcorn! It was so good. It arrived in the nick of time as I was about in a cookie/popcorn seizure. Thank you! Thank you! Thank you!
Love, Mary E.

November 20, 1990
Dear Grandma,
 Thank you so much for sending cookies! The other ladies in my tent say to tell you thank you, too! I was lucky that Mom and Grandma sent a box and it arrived yesterday, so I felt no remorse in sharing cookies! Ha! Mary and her cookie stash!
 I loved your letter as well. It seems so strange that you already have snow. Is your rainy spell going to spill over into winter giving you a lot of snow? I am morosely wondering what the weather will turn out to be like on New Year's Eve. I'm wondering what my wedding day would have been like. Hindsight being 20/20, I am so glad that Jason and I eloped. At least we have had sometime together as man and wife.
 I find myself very hungry for things you just can't send like fresh veggies and milk. I sure could go for a giant salad supper!
 It sounds like Dad is enjoying my car even though it isn't a big old Buick. It makes me want to laugh, thinking of him tooling around in a little two-seater sports car!

The oil fires in Kuwait caused the darkened sky.

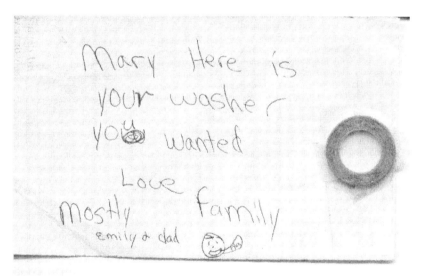

A little humor from the family.

Digging drainage ditches on my birthday.

Jason with his M16.

Homecoming.

Jason sitting on a captured Iraqi tank.

Mom (Connie McFarland) at a support rally in Fredricksburg.

Engagement picture.

1st anniversary.

My truck #201. My M-16, flak vest, gas mask and kevlar.

Well, I got to go quickly. Sounds like we have some business to take care of. Thanks again, Grandma. I love and miss you!
Love, Mary E.

November 20, 1990
Dear Jason,

Just a quick note to let you know there has been a change in plans and I am off on a mission. I'll write again when I can, do not know it's length.
Love, Mary E.

November 22, 1990
Dear Jason,

Sure miss you now, but I am so glad I got to stop at your site today on the way back from our mission. I still can't get over our luck in being able to celebrate Thanksgiving together. Luck really was with us today in more ways than one. Everybody left back here got stuck on details. Isn't that a funny twist of fate? I am doubly glad I was there with you! I've never been so glad to have gone on a mission. I do have a lot to be thankful for today and especially for your LT giving us a few private moments in his tent. I will savor your kisses for days and days to come.

I've got guard duty tomorrow. Twelve hours of complete and total boredom. I hope I get a friendly person. Sergeant V is sure in a bad mood I asked her a question and she nearly took my head off. I guess she's not used to her day being interrupted by details.

Sergeant E offered to run with me tomorrow during PT. I would like to run alone but I suppose he and the LT think I need an escort. I hate running with others-except you of course.

I prayed really hard tonight especially about the part where the Arabs solve this crap on their own and we get to go home. I told Him we didn't have to be home for Christmas but knowing we were going soon would be acceptable. Isn't that just like me? I get so many orders all day long that I think I can start ordering around the Lord. I don't think it works like that. Where is my contrite heart and repentant soul? Well, as you and the Lord must know, I love you very much but like me, I don't think you or the Lord ever get tried of hearing it, so I love you and God Bless us.
Love, Mary E.

November 25, 1990
Dear Jason,

I haven't written for a couple of days because I wasn't sure if I was coming or going with all the details I've been on. I had the worst luck after having the best luck on Thanksgiving. I pulled crap detail the day after Thanksgiving. All that extra food people ate has gone straight through them! Cans that are normally 1/3 full were brimming to the top! Oh. it was an all day affair trying to get that stuff to burn. We finally gave up and dug a pit to dump it in. I know that is highly discouraged, but there was just too much! By the time we were finished with that, I had to go straight on guard duty. Oh, did I yearn for a shower all stinking nightlong. My own stench kept me awake to be sure.

Today, I had the Chief of Staff detail at 2:30pm (and again tomorrow morning at 6:00am.) That consists of filling hand washers at the officer latrines and a garbage run. Then I had to go with Sergeant E to the motor pool to dispatch my truck. I like how it's my truck when work has to be done, but Bat-D's when it's time to go to the PX. Anyway, the darn thing wouldn't start, so we had to replace the battery. As I was carrying the battery, acid leaked out all over me. As soon as I could, I took the uniform off and stuffed the trousers in a bucket I borrowed and let them soak in some water. I asked for some time to go shower, just in case. When I took my uniform out, there were holes everywhere! Sergeant W thinks I will be able to get them patched at the laundry, but I won't be able to wear them anywhere around other units. She says we can try to get them replaced. I figure that is pretty doubtful since I never did get desert boots issued to me. What a mess, and it will be hard going with only one desert uniform!

Earlier, I went running with Sergeant W and another woman she knows. Sergeant W's friend is getting ready to go to the Sergeant Major Academy. She and Sergeant W whooped my butt. I didn't feel like running. I'm still pooped from guard duty. You know me, when I don't feel like doing something not only do my feet drag, but everything attached above my feet. At least my will power was strong enough to actually go though with it.

We are starting the new training schedule tomorrow. Organized PT three times a week and Dave is in charge of our training all week. I'm next week so send me some good ideas for what to do. I thought of maybe going over some Arabic numbers since I taught myself those and actually have read them and also getting my medic detail friend to come speak. Ideas please. This might be my chance to show up Dave for once.

I sure miss you. Mail is getting slow again. I did get another homework assignment back from Iowa–yes it was an A! I'm never quite satisfied with my haul of mail, am I? At least I'm not as bad as Sergeant V. She is such a whiner today. She was just moaning about the mail when she's gotten three packages and a bunch of letters.

We are still trying to work out our delicate situation with her. I don't know what her aversion to showering is. Well, yes I do. I know the water is cold, but we all endure. In the evenings when we all put our little cans of water on the stove to warm them for spit bathes, she puts her water on and never uses it. It was so bad the other day that Sergeant W begged off an orange from the mess truck and hung the peels in the tent to cover the smell. It is hard situation, no one wants to offend her, but she is certainly beginning to offend us.

Well, I can't really think of much else for tonight, but that I love and miss you so very very much!

Love, Mary E.

November 26, 1990

Dear Mom, Grandma and Grandpa,

Thanks for the paper. What? You were tired of reading letters on MRE box postcards? I just want to let you know I did get manage to get my hands on some real paper so the next batch of letters you get are legible. I have also sent a letter off to the *Fredericksburg Review* thanking them for remembering both Jason and me.

I got a letter from Uncle Jim, too. It sure is nice of him to write to me. I know he knows first hand how important mail call is! He told me the story of how you sent him a pillow for his foxhole during World War II and about how bad he felt to leave it behind. Just to let you know, I don't need a pillow. I use my protective mask. In it's cover it makes an acceptable pillow and no doubt that it is close at hand if I should need it!

Thanks again for the box. I was able to save some of the cookies to take to Jason when I got to see him on Thanksgiving. He opened the box and said, "These are Grandma Stong cookies!" He sure liked them! The mail is so very slow. It seems strange, but the packages seem to come faster than letters.

Yes, Mom, we are still in tents on cots with outdoor "facilities." It's like one extended Girl Scout camp trip!
Love, Mary E.

November 26, 1990
Dear Jason,
I hate this place! Nothing more to say.
Love, Mary E.

November 27, 1990
Dear Jason,

Last night after a particularly rotten day, the LT, Sergeants W, V, K and I waited in line for over four hours for fifteen minutes of free phone time. It was worth it though. I called Dad first. It was funny, Emily answered the phone and the operator says "free AT&T call from Saudi Arabia." Emily dropped the phone and screams, "Can we accept a free call from Saudi Arabia?" I was practically screaming at the phone myself, "Somebody get on the phone–it's free!" I told him about the letter I received about the rented chair accidentally being put in our storage and he also said he already used our checkbook to pay for our last phone bill. I hated wasting precious phone minutes on business like stuff, but at least we know where we stand. He told me the Iowa Hawkeyes lost their football game against Minnesota but they are still going to the Rose Bowl vs. Washington. What a honeymoon it could have made, Ha!

Dad also asked if we'd made a decision about keeping or selling the MR2. I told him I really didn't know. I hate to pay for a car we aren't driving but can't we afford to keep paying for it so it will be there when we get back? My vote is to keep it. You are much more financially smart so whatever you decide is fine. If you get a chance, write my dad and let him know.

Anyway, I split my call time in half so I could call Mom too. When the operator spoke to Mom, she literally screamed, "Mary? Oh I love you so much!" I thought she was going to cry right then and there! Oh it was a good day! Talking to Mom and Dad. I sure hope you get to use the phone on your allotted time.

I guess we've got Christmas presents on the way... ooooo?? Do you want to wait and share them? Do you think there is any chance we would even see each other at Christmas? I suppose we

can't plan a thing and whatever happens, happens. I sure love you! Please don't work too hard and BE CAREFUL!
Love, Mary E.

P.S. Well, that seems like days ago – what a busy day but I like it that way. It makes them go fast. It's 8:00pm and I'm just now getting time to finish! It sure was great to bump into you on the supply run. It was just icing and a cherry to an already good day! Every time I see you it just gives such joy and it strengthens me. As long as I have you nothing really bad can happen!

Let's see after we saw you, we came back and unloaded the truck blah, blah, blah. We finished about 1:30pm. The Chaplain is putting together a Christmas program and there was a Christmas Messiah choir practice at 2:00pm so I sang until 4:30pm. It was a lot of fun. One lady couldn't carry a tune in a bucket but it really didn't matter. We were certainly making a joyful noise!

After singing, it was back to reality. I washed some "undies" and went for a run. Sergeant E still won't let me go by myself and since Sergeant K and W had all ready gone, I was stuck with Davy. He's ok. He talked a lot which was good. It took my mind off how much I hate running in sand. Then I showered and went to eat. It was yucky chili mac! But, I was hungry since I hadn't eaten all day. I ate with your Sergeant, who has been sent here as a liaison. He's such a lost soul over here. He's back in the guys' tent now, I presume they are playing Spades again.

I've been reading some letters and I made myself a "Go Hawks" sign. I think I did rather well! Hope you can see it some time. Now it's time for my letter writing, I'm afraid I don't have anything to send you. Our mess hall is pretty skimpy lately and no packages either. It was nice not to have detail today, besides the supply run. I've got guard tomorrow. I suppose you do too. I only wish we could have it together. What fun we would have keeping each other warm. What a nice thought to end my day, You. Take care love of my life and get some rest.
Love, Mary E.

November 28, 1990
Dear Jason,

Just another exciting day in Yippeskippyville SA/USA. In all honesty, I don't feel so hot. I kept my promise and I have gone to sick call. Apparent inner ear infection not serious blah, blah, blah.

Davy gave an excruciatingly boring class this morning. I thought I was nauseous from his class, but I guess it was really the ear. I'm getting ready to go on guard duty. Can you read with NVGs on? If not, I might just turn on my flashlight. Light discipline be damned. Maybe I can write letters with NVGs tonight. I hope it's possible. I'll need something to keep me awake. You may notice a slight attitude problem today–I guess it's because I'm not feeling well and I am tired.

Last night I went to make another phone call. I wanted to talk to the grandparents. I got through to my Grandpa but Grandma was out at Home Study Club. I think I talked to Grandpa more than I ever have, on the phone that is. It sounds like they have sent you a pretty good package. He sure loves you. He kept asking about you and says you write good letters. Then, I tried to call Grandma McFarland but no answer. I suppose she was at Club too. So, I called your folks. I just babbled on. I was so tired I hardly remember what I said to them. I do remember they said if I get to see you to tell you hi and that they love you. I guess they have sent you and me some packages. They also said they wished you could write more but realize that you must be terribly busy. Yeah, you could say that, huh?

Oh! I got a care package from the Fredericksburg AmVets post #90, did you? I hope so because I don't have anything small enough to enclose in your letter. I guess I could send you some antibiotics but I really think I need to keep them myself. Sorry. Doesn't mean I don't love you. I do! I do! I do!
Love, Mary E.

November 28 or 29, 1990
Dear Jason,

Can't see the time so I don't really know what day it is. No promises you will be able to read this, as you know, I'm on guard duty. It's colder than a witch in a brass bra up here. We are on the top of a ridge and the wind blows right into this hole that is suppose to pass as a guard point. You can actually see better outside than in the hole and so we spend most of shift outside.

Well, I have to tell you of a most amazing incident tonight. Sergeant E and Davy brought me hot chocolate a little while ago. I'm not sure what surprised me more, the fact that they walked all the way out to this point or that the hot chocolate was real home mixed and not MRE crap! I am so bewildered, grateful and happy they did. It feels so cold and this wind just blows and blows. It makes my ears hurt to listen to it on and on. Yes, I am keeping my ear covered as best I can, and yes, I have taken my antibiotics. Bye for now.

Later: I gave up writing in the dark last night. I couldn't manage it between the light, the wind and duty. To my amazement, my surprises just seem to keep coming. We had a real breakfast this morning. What a treat after guard last night to eat scrambled eggs and fried potatoes. It was pretty good stuff! I slept pretty well having a nice full belly and nice warming sleeping bag. Not much more to say, but I love you and miss you so much!

Love, Mary E.

December 2, 1990
Dear Dad,

I've had a pretty busy week. My Sergeant puts one of us "in charge" for a week and my week starts tomorrow. So, in between last week's training and other daily tasks, I've been trying to prepare a good training schedule. So far it looks good on paper. I guess it remains to be seen how well it will work in reality.

Yes, I would say the general feeling over here is although we are getting tired of the sit and wait scenario, we are supportive of what President Bush is doing. Yes, sometimes I wonder why we are here, but I think it's best we stop the fruitcake before he gets more powerful and nukes somebody. I have heard some awful reports coming out of Kuwait and if they are even half true, this aggression needs to be neutralized. So, here we are.

Don't send any videotapes, Dad. We don't have any access to a VCR. I know some units do have them, but not us. Oh yes, you had asked about showers. Yes, we have a shower, for now. I would guess the only guys that don't are at really remote locations. We knew that could happen to us at anytime so, we built our own "travel" shower back at Fort Hood, but it still takes water. Right now we have to haul our water in five-gallon cans to the shower point and the water is icy cold, but it is cleansing.

I wish I could have talked longer, but I needed to call Mom too. I waited in line for four hours! It was the middle of our night too, but it was worth it! I love and miss you all so much.

Love, Mary E.

December 2, 1990
Dear Jason,
    The moon is so large. I've been howling at it for you, well, at least in my mind. You know it's a little scary but I was thinking that supper would have been pretty good tonight if it wasn't so lonely without you. You are my best friend and I miss sharing everything with you. I trust you with all my thoughts and feelings. I trust you so completely. It's so nice to sit in church and think how fortunate I am to have you in my life. There are too many people here that are going to have regrets and I am so glad not to be one of them. You make me complete even when we are apart and your love sustains me.
Love, Mary E.

December 7, 1990
Dear Uncle Jim,
    I so often think of you on this day. I know you weren't at Pearl Harbor, but it certainly sent you down a long and winding road. Hopefully, I have had my first and last Thanksgiving over here. It was so nice of all the family to each send letters of the accounts of Thanksgiving. My Dad and Grandma McFarland wrote of their Thanksgiving. Meanwhile, Mom and Grandma Stong wrote of their Thanksgiving, and Susan told me about both. All accounts sounded very nice. I trust you had a good holiday too and didn't spend too much time worrying about us over here.
    I have been going to a Bible study and at our last meeting the chaplain was very upset. He is being sent back to Fort Hood. He is to start another church for the families back home. He believes he would be of more value over here. I told him, "There is something good in everything." My dad has been telling me that for years, and he would probably be surprised to know I had actually listened to him. The whole study group seemed to grasp hold of the idea as we spent the rest of our time finding positives and proving the theory.
    My section teases me by saying I'm the only person they know that can have social life in the desert. It stems from me going to Bible study on Wednesday night, church on Sunday morning and choir practice when I can. Our tent always seems to have visitors too. Is that what you call Iowa hospitality or Grandma's cookies?

According to the Chaplain, Iowa is sending a flag and some boxes for Iowans. The Chaplain and I have been searching for other Iowans to share it with, but so far I have only found one other Iowan.

Well, you take care

Love, Mary E.

December 7, 1990

Dear Jason,

I hope this letter will eventually reach you. I know you have left your old site. I know you will be ok wherever it is you have gone. I hope it is farther south. I know you guys will take care of each other and hopefully this won't last much longer.

I have to write and tell of our excitement around here. Our very own Sergeant R lost it big time! For lack of better term, he snapped over a shower! I was sitting over in the guys' tent. We were going over some training schedules. I didn't give Sergeant R too much thought as he draped his towel over his shoulder and grabbed his shower kit. A little while later he came rushing back in, kind of muttering to himself in Spanish like he does when he's pissed. He grabbed an ammo can and used his bayonet to break the metal band, opened the can and grabbed a clip and ran. He did all of this so fast it didn't really register with us at first as to what he had taken. Meanwhile, he locked and loaded on these poor guys that were just repairing the shower tank and threatened to shoot them if they wouldn't let him take a shower! Thank goodness Sergeants E and T took off after him so he didn't get a shot off. They subdued him until the MPs hauled his freaked-out butt away! That could have been bad.

He came back later with an MP escort to collect his belongings. They took him up to another site where he will have a physco-evaluation. I heard he could get up to five years in jail and court-martial. Wow, fifteen years in down the drain over a shower. Yes, pun intended! Pretty scary when you actually think about it!

I know I've been a little mad at Sergeant R ever since he tried to trade me for camels the one time we met locals on a supply run. I know he thought it was a funny joke, but I don't think the Saudi thought it was a joke. Now what kind of explaining would he have done if that guy had showed back up with five camels in tow? Still, I wouldn't wish any ill to him! Freaky.

Well, I'm wishing on every star I can that we will be together soon, safe and sound! I love you!
Love, Mary E.

December 7, 1990
Dear Mom,

Thank you! I got the present box last night along with one from Dad and one from my in-laws. I do wish they wouldn't all come at the same time, but don't get me wrong I am so grateful!

Jason has moved. I don't know where. I am thinking they moved farther south, which is great because he is farther away from Kuwait. The bad part is I don't know when I will ever see him again.

I've been trying to keep busy here to make the time go faster. I still miss you very much and love you too!
Love, Mary E.

December 8, 1990
Dear Dad,

I just wanted to let you know I received two letters from you and a package from the hospital. I am very appreciative but wasn't sure who was responsible so I just sent a thank you to the return address. Hopefully someone will get it and pass my thanks along.

I had guard duty last night and the sunrise this morning was really beautiful. The colors were especially vibrant. Yes, I know, "There is something good in everything." Nothing much more to report, I just wanted to let you know the letters and package arrived.
Love, Mary E.

December 9, 1990
Dear Iowans,

Hey! Hey! Hey! It's Iowa day! No, not the place they grow potatoes that's Idaho. No, not Ohio – I said IOWA! The land of "Our Liberties we prize! Our rights we will maintain!" Thank you to the Governor and his "helpers" for the flag and for the boxes. Although we may have been few in numbers, we were large in pride. The chaplain, who by the way is jealous since he is from Minnesota, had us out in the compound asking everyone, "are you from Iowa?" He would crack jokes about the Golden Gopher in charge of the Hawkeyes.

It was really great. I'm so proud to be from Iowa anyway, but boy, this was the "topper." No one else's state has done what you've done Iowa. Thank you! I feel very proud to be an Iowan and it makes the time I spend over here that much more worth while. It's my duty, does anyone really need more explanation than that for why we are here?

People say they are tired of sitting and waiting. Yes, I can see that point, but I know that there are still only twenty-four hours in a day and how you spend those hours is your choice.

Maybe this is just a big learning experience for us all not to be so dependant on our conveniences and contraptions. I found the key! The more I do in a day, the faster that day goes. I have been reading and writing, taking army classes, and college classes besides the regular training and the details and personal projects and even answering any person mail. I still seem to run out of time everyday.

I just finally decided it's not worth moping about thinking doom is right over our heads. This place is miserable enough. There's something good in everything. Say it with me, "There's something good in everything." I am trying my best to adopt this belief of my dad's. So, if you get a letter from your loved one or even just decide to write any soldier, gently tell him or her to look for the something good. Send a long a book and ask them to write back. See, there; three more things to add to the day!

Love, Mary E.

December 14, 1990
Dear Dad,

I had a twelve hour guard shift last night and spent my time trying to come up with the answer to the question, "What's it like over there?" I have tried to use an example we all can identify with, but you'll still need to use you imagination.

So, imagine Interstate 80 between Iowa City and Des Moines. It's probably snow covered by now. The snow is sand. Blizzards are dust storms and plows are needed to keep the sand off the highway. The exits don't exist and neither do most of the farms. Only the towns visible from the road exist and all the cattle you see are camels. Of course, the snow is hot sand that doesn't melt.

The speed limit is 120 kph and it's a two-lane highway where turn signals aren't for turning. They are used to signal if it's safe to pass or not. There are no passing lines, pass when you want to and if someone is coming flash your lights so they slow down and so you can finish your pass. Oh, not to mention the right side is legal to pass on too. Well, you've just passed your first driving lesson. How about a standing lesson? You need to familiarize yourself with the standing and no standing zones, not to mention standing where it's legal on odd or even days. I am not kidding. These are posted signs!

Naturally, these lessons are geared toward men only. Women are another subject. Women are only allowed to ride in the back seat of a car here. Driving is completely forbidden. I'm not sure if you heard about the women who drove themselves to the capital, Riyadh. Some of the women were executed and the rest imprisoned. I cannot fathom such constraints and punishments. Neither can I understand that mentality. But then, I guess I don't have to. I am a guest in this country and I do not intend on staying.

Unless a thumbs up is a curse in Saudi Arabia, the Arabians seem pleased to have us here. The men honk and wave along with thumbs up where ever we go. The children are so animated as they flock around our trucks while asking in their broken universal English words of "Pepsi?" "Candy?" The little girls are unveiled and laugh and smile with their dark curls tumbling and mischievous eyes flashing. For an all to brief moment in their lives, they are equal to their brothers. I look at those girls and wonder what will become of them. Will they all become a faceless black veil with only sullen eyes peering out at world they can only minimally take part in? It is not for me to say, but I will just the same. I think that is wrong. Very wrong. Mostly we are out in the middle the desert and don't see much of the culture or countrymen, but in passing. I think perhaps that is just as well in this situation.

Camels seem much less interested in these bothersome soldiers that have increased the annoying traffic. They cross the road whenever and wherever they please. Can you believe they don't use the camel crossing signs? As if a camel could read any better than the deer at home do! One day while driving, I had to bring the truck to a complete halt while a camel slowly plodded across the road. He stopped in front of me and looked up as if to say, "Yeah? What do ya want? It's my desert!" Camels seem to be the nicest animal out here. Snakes bite, scorpions sting, and even the plants are mean and prickly!

I have been wondering if the people of Saudi Arabia love their country's view like we in Iowa do. I know riding my horse back in the timber of the farm I used to sigh and think, "Boy, this is beautiful!" I miss the smell of the dark rich soil after it has just been plowed. I miss the sweet smell of freshly cut alfalfa. I miss the fresh clean and cool feel of the breeze after a thunderstorm blows over. I just wonder if people here feel the same about this place.

I used to think that this place was the ugliest place I had ever been. I started thinking that I should work harder on finding something good in everything. Well, Saudi had extraordinary sunrises and sunsets. The stars are clear and sparkling and the moon glows bright and dazzling.

One morning after guard duty the sky was just gorgeous. There were some rare clouds blurring the sun and the light spread across the sky contrasting the livid blues of the sky with the ever-growing warm orange glow of the sun. It stopped me in my tracks and I just stared and simply stated, "Wow!"

There is certainly nothing to get in the way of seeing beautiful sunsets. The sun is a huge fiery globe that dips behind the dunes that for one fleeting moment I can envision as the undulating waves of a cornfield drifting in the evening breeze of Iowa. As you should well know, for every sunrise there must be a sunset, thus we have at least two beautiful moments a day here.

The stars on a night without the moon are incredible. Second only to summer nights on the farm. If I strain my ears hard enough I can make myself believe I can hear the incessant croaking of the bullfrogs out at the pond, dappled with an occasional beller of the cows in the county line pasture. It does seem unnaturally quiet here. It is hard to gauge how far a sound has traveled and if it was a real sound or something you just believed you heard.

I, of course, have been wishing on every falling star I see. After all, if it works for Jiminy Cricket, why not for me? Those stars are often the backdrop and topic of the late night hours of guard duty. After you and the other guard have talked about every conceivable facet of home. There will be a lull in the conversation as the two of you sigh and gaze at the multitudes of stars, and you think for one brief moment, "This isn't such a bad place." Then reality floods back and you realize just how much you miss home. And I really, really do.

Love, Mary E.

December 15, 1990
Dear Mom,

It's 11:30pm on a Saturday night and it is way past my bedtime. My friends from the University of Iowa would probably be thinking, "Ready for bed? Why, that's the time you used to go out!" Ben Franklin may have said, "Early to bed, early to rise makes a man (woman) healthy, wealthy and wise," but all I know is early to bed when one had to rise early just plain makes one less grumpy!

I'll risk looking a little sleepy at the 7:30am worship service. After all, 7:30am is sleeping in and it is Saturday night! I was thinking, what would the look on the pastor's face be if I walked into church carrying my M16A2 rifle? For a soldier, your M16 and your protective mask are your best friends and constant companions. Since the day I left Fort Hood, the three of us haven't been a part. Really! We carried them on the plane, where they were set at our feet while we flew. I take them to the latrine, where there is a nail conveniently located in front of each hole. I take them to the shower, where you place the weapon across the top of the dividers and hang the mask from the rifle. Most importantly, I sleep with them both. Everyday, every single day, I clean the dust off and out of them. See what I mean? Constant buddies. Don't ever get caught without them or worse yet, never dare leave them or lose them!

So, naturally we take them to church with us. I can imagine the first Sunday Jason and I are home in the States getting ready to leave for church and instead of, "Honey? Where's my purse?" It will be, "Honey? Where's my protective mask?"

You'd think it would be hard to remember to take them everywhere, but actually if you are without them it's strange. I guess in a place like this you just don't forget. It's almost like forgetting to put your shirt and pants on before you leave for work.

I have become so "attached" to my weapon, that I have given it a name and I'm not the only one to name their weapon. Since my M16 was made in Connecticut, and I believe that's where Prudential Insurance Company is based, my weapon is named Prudential. I can't think of any better life insurance than my M16A2. Well, at least in this environment! There is a very good saying, "Stay alert, stay alive." Well, I've got to go.
Love, Mary E.

December 16, 1990

Dear Dad,

Thank you for the box! The popcorn was great. Oh yes, thanks for the washer! Although, it wasn't quite the kind of washer I was wanting, I will hold on to it. One never knows in these parts when you'll have a stray bolt in need of washer. Next time I will be clearer with my requests for a magic *washing machine* instead of a washer!

I got to visit Jason and he got his boxes the day before. It was so nice to see him! They had moved, but then they came back and will be moving again today. Doesn't sound very promising for seeing him on Christmas.

Someone sent a cross-stitch kit in the any soldier mail. I picked it up and have been working on it to give or maybe send to Jason for Christmas. I remember thinking last Christmas, as I sat on duty, that next Christmas would be better. Well, maybe three times is a charm and next Christmas will be better and possibly white. I can only hope!

Boy, what I'd give for a snow day right now! I remember looking out the back door of Mom's house trying to gauge if there was enough snow blowing around to stay up late or not. I have no trouble keeping busy between all the training, details and keeping all the letters from home answered. I'm sick of the situation here, but never bored.

We ran across a little pit viper the other day. It is hard to imagine something so small could be so deadly. There are some people over here keeping scorpions as pets. They fix them up a little home in a water bottle with sand and actually "play" with them. Bizarre!

No, Dad, I am not taking any pictures over here, because I don't have a camera. I'm not sure there is anything about this place that I really want to remember that clearly. Thanks for asking.

Love, Mary E.

P.S. Martha, I can't believe you sent that old school picture of mine to Jason! Just wait until you get married. I already have several good ones in mind for your future husband! Jason really got a good kick out of it so I guess I won't hold it over you this time.

December 16, 1990

Dear Linda,

I know how you feel. When we were first put on alert, everyone was scared not knowing anything, thinking we were leaving tomorrow, but then things slowed down and I thought it would all blow over before we ever got here. Then we took the trucks to the port, but there were rumors all the time, until finally I didn't believe I was going until I was on the plane!

Some packing suggestions would be long johns, a sheet for warm nights like at the port and a blanket for the desert. This is certainly a land of extremes! I would suggest at least two sets of exercise clothes. That way you have one for exercise and one to sleep in. Sweats take forever to dry, especially near the water.

A burner would be a smart idea, but I'm not sure where you would find the fuel for it. Hot water for washing would sure be nice. It would be nice for heating soup or making hot chocolate, or in your case, tea. Logistics/supply has been pretty good so far for things like soap, deodorant, laundry soap and female stuff. We brought quite a bit with us just in case, but anything we have needed hasn't been too hard to come by. Unless you want something special because supply is your basic of basic stuff.

Hair gets really, really dry in the desert and skin too. Closer to the port and water, it's not so bad, but the closer to water, the worse the flies are. The most important items over here are powder, wet wipes and a bowl for washing! Supply doesn't carry many wet wipes, and the PX can't stock enough. Ideally you could take two bowls, one for washing up in and a larger one for laundry, but I seem to be doing ok with just one, but at all cost definitely pack a bowl of some kind!

If you still have some extra room, I would pack some kind of bag to take all your shower stuff around in and shower shoes. The showers are a pretty long walk away, and the pallets used as floors are kind of nasty. I've never had trouble with my feet until now. I use Sea Breeze applied with cotton balls. I'd use foot powder if I could lay my hands on some.

Garbage bags are good for after shower to step on and when you get back to the tent and then you can pick them up and shake them out until next time. Also if you are going to be in a tent try to take something for a floor. Some sort of canvass would be good. But then, with you being an officer, they would probably right out issue you a wood floor.

I would be lost with out my Walkman for at lest getting some news. We can get Armed Forces Radio. They have AP network news with a wide variety of music. Of course, bring some extra batteries! Although I would imagine you might be near a regular style PX, the baby PXs we have in the back of a semi don't usually have any batteries. Candles are good for saving on flashlight batteries if you don't have electricity, but the do make me nervous.

If your glasses have plastic lens, see if you can get them covered with that coating to prevent scratches. The sand just eats plastic lens. Remember your sunglasses. They are invaluable.

Naturally, I'm not sure where you would be sent with the Navy. There has been a really large Navy M*A*S*H type site located near by. You can sure tell where they are at night. Apparently, the Navy doesn't abide by the same light discipline standards as we do.

I am assuming you would be by the port on, or near, the hospital ships. I doubt you would have any trouble procuring any thing you would need. Mid-desert, the story is a little harder, but then I'm an enlisted and you are an officer and that in it's self is a HUGE difference. That is probably a bigger difference than just Army versus Navy.

Good Luck! I just hope you won't have to be deployed.

Love, Mary E.

December 22, 1990
Dear Dad,

Thank you so very, very much for the box. It was a real winner. Christmas is right around the corner, but it doesn't make me sad because Christmas is a heartfelt holiday, and no matter where or who you are with, your spirit and soul is celebrating along with God on Jesus' birthday.

What does make me sad, depressed and miserable is my leadership and co-workers. I knew before coming over here the amount of prejudice and backstabbing that can go on in the Army, but I, unfortunately, have been experiencing it first hand. I am still waiting to be promoted, but it seems as though I have just as much chance of being demoted by my Sergeant. He seems to believe along the lines of the Saudis, that women have no purpose to exist. He can't stand the thought, let alone believe there could be a woman with intelligence and industrious thinking.

This is the same one that has been giving me grief since day one. It's a very long drawn out story that I won't waste space relating. I have been put on a different team, so hopefully things will look better. I'm afraid feeling so stifled and stomped on has put a damper on my emotions and writing. In fact, this is my first real attempt to write letters longer than acknowledging I have received a correspondence. I know that I must persevere. After all, I am a McFarland by blood, and I have been bred better than that. I can endure individuals wasting their lives in the quicksand of ignorance and single-mindedness, and I will rise above and be an even better person, while they sink to the lowest depth of mental stagnation.

Anyway, again, thanks so much for the box. I hope I can carry it all with me. Hint! I'll be very busy in the next and coming weeks, so if you don't hear from me you'll know why.

Love, Mary E.

December 22, 1990
Dear Mom, Grandma and Grandpa,

Thanks for the letter, Mom! Thanks for the box! It was very yummy! It didn't really hit me what I was missing back home until I ate the cookies. Simply the taste of your special recipe cookies, Grandma, and I was transported home. The snow was gently falling as we were digging through the boxes of lights and garland searching for the red felt Rudolf. The Christmas music plays quietly on your stereo consol while I ceremonially place Rudolf on top of the TV, officially signaling the start of the holiday decoration free for all. Thank you! Thank you, for bringing all those good memories back to me.

We had another bad sandstorm. They are just like blizzards. The sand comes in the tent and I've learned to cover everything with a plastic bag so I can shake it out when the wind calms down.

Well, nothing else to report. Sorry my letters have been so short. We've been really busy. Thanks again for the letters and the wonderful box. I love and miss you heaps and heaps!

Love, Mary E.

December 25, 1990
Dear Family,

Ah! Christmas, what a day to reflect on PEACE! Actually, after attending a small Christmas concert by the 1st Cav band, eating the best meal I've had out here yet and not getting on any detail, I declared Christmas a success. The only thing that could have made it better would have been a visit from Jason.

I settled down in my tent, hiding from the "shmall" (dust storm) with a little weather induced free time. I started going through the newspapers Dad sent me and a picture caught my eye. It made me laugh! The pictures showed two students holding posters one saying, "Let the sanctions work!" and the other "Honk for the U.S. out of the Middle East!" Isn't that contradiction? Were those two protesting on the same side? So, I was compelled to read the article about it being vogue to protest.

Now, doesn't it seem that if we let the sanctions work, I will have to stay over here longer. That picture made me stop and turn back to the first part with a picture of 600 marchers so I could read their signs. So, here are a few opinions from a G.I.

To the guy with the sign that reads, "A life – it's a terrible thing to waste." Yes, I agree, and that's why I personally believe kids shouldn't drop out of school, people shouldn't do drugs, and that's why I'm over here risking my life, so hopefully you and the ones with the "It's an Arab problem" sign don't get drafted when in a couple of years Hussein sends a nuclear bomb over to the United States, or some direct attack suddenly makes it our problem. Lastly, to the person suggesting this is strictly over oil, it's not. I've seen some things I don't want to ever see again, trust me on this one.

Thank you, I have just utilized what makes our country great– the ability to express my feelings, as well as the protesters to express their opinions. I believe that is an important factor for me to hold on to as I sit in the desert. I love my freedom. I love my country, and I have chosen to protect it by service of my country. Don't get me wrong–I can't wait to get back, but there is a job to be done and it's my job to do it.

All I ask of anyone is before passing judgment on any topic is to weigh both sides of the issue. Try to put yourself in the other guy's shoes. For example in this case, as a pro-sanction supporter sits in front of the television waiting for the sanctions to work, try to imagine sitting on a cot during a dust storm away from your family.

Unfortunately, not every solution to a problem is perfect. Sometimes you've got to give some to take some. My history teacher had a good idea to make a list, one side for the pros and the other side for the cons, or perhaps advantages/disadvantages. Which side is

longer or which side tallies more points? Ultimately, the choice is
yours. Aren't you glad you have a choice? Aren't you glad you can
express your choice? That is your right as an American, how
fortunate for you!

Boy, have I really rattled on expressing my own opinions! So,
Merry Christmas to everyone and joy upon you all.
Love, Mary E.

December 25, 1990
Dear Husband, love of my life,

Seeing you was a miracle I was beginning to believe was not
going to happen. When you walked into my tent in the middle of that
sandstorm, I thought you *were* a mirage and I found myself
wondering if perhaps you were a mirage after you had to leave so
quickly. But you, my love, and your sweet kisses were the best
Christmas present I could have ever received. I will never forget your
Christmas gift. A yo-yo has more significance in this place with its
roller coast ride of emotions than you will ever know. Please don't be
sorry about the gift. I truly love it, and it means so much to me. I
thank God for granting me the opportunity to hold you in my arms
today, however briefly. You are my life, my world, my everything
and I love you more than I could ever try to put on paper. Thank you!
Thank you for coming into my life, for accepting the woman that I am
and loving me. You are so precious to me and I love you so. Take
care, my sweet love. Until we are reunited, I pledge my everlasting
devotion to you.
Love, Your wife

December 26, 1990
Dear Mom,

No Christmas tree this year?? What a bummer! Wish I could
have been there to help you get it down from the attic. Maybe I'll buy
you a brand new tree for next year! I'll move all of my horses and
stuffed animals and books out of my old room so you can store it
right in there, and you won't ever have to depend on someone
climbing that rickety old ladder to the attic to get it down. No arguing,
my mind is set.

I was just thinking if that crazy man wouldn't have been so
stupid, Jason and I would be home with you right now! Well, I guess
I shouldn't think about it. We had a sand storm, no, a sand blizzard

yesterday. It was about 4:30pm and I was so sad and low because I thought Jason wasn't coming. I had wished on so many stars, said so many prayers. I didn't think there was anyway he couldn't come. But the clock kept ticking by. I was getting lower and lower. I started rethinking my decision to drop out of the Messiah choir. The choir was traveling from site to site giving Christmas concerts and I didn't want to be gone from this site if Jason would show up, so I quit. Here I was thinking, "I should have stayed in the choir, because perhaps I would have ended up at his site." When who should come blowing into my tent with a sandy gust but Jason!

I only got to see him for ten minutes, but what a fabulous ten minutes! I made him a cross stitch that read "Family + Friends = Love". I had also found a book about General Patton that someone had sent to any soldier. He gave me a yo-yo and some wet wipes, but he was really the present I had been hoping for! Oh Mom, I love him so much. I don't know that I could have stood the day without seeing him. There are times when I think I am just going to burst with the ache of missing him. This too shall pass, I know…I know.

So, tell me about your Christmas at Grandma and Grandpa's. We had turkey, roast, ham, sweet potatoes, mashed potatoes, stuffing, gravy and pie, and oh yes, eggnog for dinner. It was pretty good for Army food. Most of it was fake or dehydrated, but acceptable by far! Compared to normal, it was a feast. My next wish is that I do NOT get put on poop burning detail tomorrow. It's gonna be a bad one!

What a Christmas! One to tell my grandchildren about. Shoot, at this rate I'm wondering if we will ever get the children? Sorry that just slipped out. I sure love and miss you, Mom. Thanks for being such a good and loving Mom. You are a pretty cool woman. I'd be glad to know you even if you weren't my Mom.
Love, Mary E.

December 28, 1990
Dear Jason,

Another day has passed with no word from you. I just hope you are o.k. I am sending more cards and stuff I received. Four of them are from a class project. Thank you for forwarding some of your interesting mail to me too.

I had guard duty last night and it got so cold. The wind blew so hard it nearly knocked me down. Some detail came along and dismantled the bunker we had built so there was no protection out there at all. I just can't get over how cold it can get here. I know that doesn't come as a shock to you.

I had duty with this guy that races motorcycles. He was full of information. I never thought I would meet someone that was as crazy about motorcycles as you. It's nice to think of life going on after this and of motorcycle races and skiing and being together.

I sure do love you and I sure do miss you. I am so glad we saw each other on Christmas. It will be nice when we can share our oatmeal together again. I think of you and me snuggling in front of fireplaces, sipping hot chocolate, and taking hot steamy bubble bathes to keep me warm through the long nights of guard duty. I'm glad I have you, at least in thought.

Love, Mary E.

December 28, 1990
Dear Mom,

I have a little more time to tell you some more about Christmas. We had a nice Christmas Eve service. It was even by candlelight, of course, a lot of things we do around here are! Then, we even went caroling from tent to tent-including the General's! After the little concert by the 1st Cav band, the Chaplain played Santa! He was really funny! He is such a bright light for so many feeling so gloomy.

Ever since the dust storm on Christmas day, it has been cold. The temperatures change so much it's hard to get use to them. Can't believe I came to the desert and I'm freezing. Sometime the sky gets really gray and I expect it to snow at anytime. Wouldn't that be crazy? Get my skis!

I sure am glad you write. I've been getting letters pretty regular now. I will sure miss it if and when the war starts. Thanks for the *Fredericksburg Review*. It was neat seeing my letter in the paper.

It's almost cozy in my tent with the potbelly stove going. Sure wish I was sharing it with Jason and not three other ladies! I love you!

Love, Mary E.

December 31, 1990
Dear Dad,

Well, what a wedding day, huh? No offense, but I really hope it blizzards. I heard on the radio that Iowa is completely shut down with temperatures of –55 F. Sshh, don't tell me the truth!

Dad, whatever you do, don't tell Mom this next part. You know what a worrywart she is! It was very scary for me and I want to tell someone, but I don't want to worry Jason either.

I went running as we have normally been doing when I had what they are calling a severe asthma attack. It was just awful! It came on really fast without any kind of warning signs. All of a sudden, I just couldn't seem to keep up, so I started to walk back to the main road. By the time I made it up to the checkpoint going into the camp, I could hardly walk and Sergeant K and W came rushing back for me and were walking on either side of me. It was getting worse and worse and I was getting weaker and nearly passed out. They practically had to carry me to the medic tent. I last clearly remember the medics running out of the tent to help. I am kind of fuzzy after that. The medics gave me a shot to help me breathe but, it didn't work. They put me on oxygen and gave me a second shot. I was so out of it Sergeant K had to fill me in on a lot of the details. I was cramping up and curling into a ball. At this point, they sent some one to grab my uniform because I was wearing PT uniform. Meanwhile they were on the radio getting ready to call in the medical helicopter. They were about to send me to the hospital when the shot finally started to help. I almost was still sent to the hospital because there weren't any doctors on site, but one arrived and so I stayed put. As much as I like helicopters, I don't think that would have been an enjoyable ride.

When it was over, I was so stiff I couldn't straighten anything out. I felt like I was being crushed into a ball. I had to have the Sergeants pry my hands back open because I just couldn't move them. The shots made me really shaky and I was freezing cold. I have two giant bruises from them as well.

Today I am so stiff and sore and still so weak. All my muscles are so tight. It is just like the time I was nearly electrocuted by the switch on the silo by the barn. I'm pretty wiped out. Things seem ten times heavier and I feel like I'm about 123 years old. I couldn't even carry a water jug. I was dragging one to use until Aaron said he couldn't take it any longer and personally escorted me back to my tent.

He has sure been a blessing. I have found a good friend in him since I joined his team. He was really worried and walked me to where I needed to go today. It must have been a pretty serious situation, because of the number of NCOs that keep stopping by the tent to see how I am.

I'm glad I can at least write today. I couldn't even pick up a pen last night. I am so disappointed by all of this. I really hate being hampered in any way, especially my physical activities. I hate to give anyone the idea that I am less than the soldier I should be. Hopefully I'll soon be back on track. I have to go back to see the Doctor on Wednesday. So, like I said, "What a wedding day."

Oh yes, Freedom Road sounds like a great name for the bull. Is he destined to be a national champion and then McFarland Hereford Farm will be on its way to financial freedom too? Hey, quit that laughing!

As for our situation, we've all stopped saying, "if the war starts" and are saying, "when the war starts." I don't see how we will be able to avoid it. I just pray harder that the plans I've heard work well and "he" really doesn't have any surprises. I think he is a mighty big "bluffer." I sure miss you!

Love, Mary E.

December 31, 1990
Dear Mom, Grandma and Grandpa,

So much for my wedding day! Once again Grandma and Grandpa, thanks for the box. I know a lot of love went into it and I sure appreciate that love!

Yes, my in-laws write quite often and have sent three boxes. My mother-in-law, Sherry, sent miniature Christmas decorations. We hung them up all over our tent. They were a nice festive touch! They have also sent several Portland postcards so I can get an idea of what the place looks like.

Please keep writing, Mom! I love and miss you so much!

Love, Mary E.

December 31, 1990
Dear Jason,

Happy Wedding Day! I thought I'd write with this purple pen I ran across in an any soldier box. Purple would have been the color of the day, so I thought it was an especially lucky find. I will be howling at our full blue moon tonight. Well, I guess in the interest of sound discipline, I'll howl silently.

It wasn't an especially good day. Our trucks are such wrecks. 201 is deadlined, 200 is deadlined, 202 is broken down at another site and 203 has been impounded along with Bill and Sergeant E at D-Rear. They have been held up for not having an officer's signature on the dispatch even though they were told they didn't need it. That leaves us with no trucks at this point. I hope your gear is in better shape than ours!

Let's hope the New Year will dawn with some good news and happy moments! Boy, this day sure isn't what I thought it would be, but then, this year hasn't been anything like I thought it would be. I never dreamed by the end of this year I would be married and in a war. Either of those would have been enough, don't you think? Well, if it is any consolation, Sergeant K said she heard on the news that Iowa is at a stand still with a blizzard and temperatures of -55 F. No velvet dress could have withstood that! I don't know if she made that up for my sake or not, but I don't want to know! I sure do love you, Sweetheart. I miss you so much and ache for your kisses especially today. I am so glad we eloped!
Love, Mary E.

January 7, 1991
Dear Grandma,

Thanks for the letter! Glad you are feeling better! I worry about all of you at home. Especially with all the cold weather. We've been having a cold spell too. Down into the 30s at night. I know that doesn't sound very cold to you in Iowa in January, but it makes for a pretty cold twelve hour guard shift. It's impossible to acclimatize to this weather. Warm, cold, warm, cold. Today was really nice, and now on guard duty I'm freezing. Thank goodness for the long johns Dad sent.

No, I don't have much contact with Saudis at all. If we need any toiletries we go to a little PX about ten miles away. It's just a semi-trailer. They sell toiletries and Army necessities and a little bit of junk food.

No, I haven't seen Jason since our quick visit on Christmas. Not really too much to tell you, Grandma. I am just anxiously waiting to come home. I'm getting tired of being a pawn in an international

chess game. I sure do love and miss you. Promise me you will take good care of yourself and I promise I will too!
Love, Mary E.

January 7, 1991
Dear Jason,
    I love you! I always have a case of the miss you's, but especially when, like now, I'm on this never ending guard duty. I look up in the sky and see the beautiful stars or the big moon and think, "No matter where we are, we are still looking at the same ones!" Just like when you went home after A.I.T. that was the very same moon we were howling at and eventually that separation ended and so will this one too! We just have to try and remember times like these will make us better and stronger than the rest. We will be more capable than the rest in everything we do! Remember, there is something good in everything! We may mot be able to see it or understand it right now-we will someday!
    Just sitting here at this guard point alone in the dark-the other chick is gone to the latrine-I just revel in the fact that you love me so much and in the realization that I am you wife. I am actually someone's wife! I never dreamed it would happen, and I thank God for letting you come into my life. I love you, trust you, want you, need you and most of all believe in us. Our separation, I think, is really teaching me things like appreciating what I've got, namely-YOU. Well, I've got all night out here so I won't seal the envelope yet.
    Good thing I didn't seal the envelope because here I am again. It's 3:00am and thank God for the heaters. I'd surely freeze with out it. Although, they do have a down side. I burned my finger on one last time I had guard. Between me being so tired and my fingers being so numb with cold, I didn't even realize it until the next day after I woke up with a nasty blister.
    Nine hours down with three more to go. I guess I'll survive this guard shift. The glow of this heater makes me dreamy thinking of a cold winter's evening and us together in front of a blazing fire. Unfortunately, the glow of the heater isn't bright enough to see by and my batteries are getting mighty dim. Besides, I can't really think of anything suitable to put on paper, just day (night) dreaming about you. Can't think of a better obsession than thinking of you. Our love is so special it could span the world infinitely…batteries dead.

Love, Mary E.

January 14, 1991
Dear Jason,
Yeah, I know – why am I writing to you when we have no mail drop? Well, I do feel closer when I do, so I'll write. Yet, it seems silly to write to you so often when I can't really write too much. I don't exactly know what is ok to say and what isn't, so I guess it's best just not say anything. (Except, sleeping with an ammo box is extremely uncomfortable, but then I'm sure you know that too!) I happened to catch enough sleep the other night to have a dream. No, it wasn't a dream, but a nightmare almost like the one I had before, but just a little different. This time instead of just me looking the sky, all of us in Bat-D were looking at the sky and every bomber and aircraft and helicopter imaginable was flying over us. This time we know they are going to Baghdad, but it's scary because we know we are in the direct path of retaliation, yet we don't know how it's going to happen or when, how, where? Reality isn't half as frightening as the anticipation. I suppose.
Love, Mary E.

January 15, 1991
Dear Jason,
Thought I would write to you since we have a mail drop now, but–well-ah-gosh I just don't have anything to say. Shocks you doesn't it? I do wish I could talk to you. I am giving you a warning. If you don't hear from me for a while–mission. Enough said.
I hope you are ok. I'm sure you're probably "missioning" too. I really hate not knowing where you are. This place was tolerable when I had a chance to see you, but now there's no chance to see you or hear from you and pretty slim to no chance of even getting mail from you. I wonder if you can even find time to write. I'm sure you're "missioned" out. Still, I never give up hope that if we get mail, a letter from you just might arrive. Until then, I'll be content to think of you 24-7. I'm sure I would dream about you to if only we had time to sleep. Please take care.
Love, Mary E.

January 16, 1991
Dear Jason,

Well, not much to say. With a deadline in the sand fast approaching, there as been a new duty assignment. We now take a twenty-four hour shift on reactionary guard. Eight of us stay in a separate tent and we have to stay there except for taking turns walking the perimeter from guard point to guard point and trips to the latrine. We would be the first notified so we could respond immediately to any threat. They do let us sleep, but we remain fully clothed including boots, mask and weapon, so we can be off at a moments notice. Of course, I'm on it. Great timing, huh? Well, I have doubts anything will ever happen. This thing won't ever get started and it will never finish. Does it seem like that to you? Although, I'm not sure if we should really wish to get the show on the road.

I know we were hoping for R&R, but forget it-won't happen. Actually, if you can take it, by all means, GO! I'm sure you need the break, but I can't go. Boy, I sure hope you're ok. The last letter I received from you was New Year's. Seems like an eternity since Christmas!

Well, I think it's stupid to fill up and waste this paper telling you how I miss you and how sad I am. Blah! Blah! Blah! I'm sure you know. I'm sure you feel it too! Sometimes it feels like I've never met you and you're just a pen pal, but then I think of the past and how wonderful our time together has been. It's the stuff that keeps me warm on guard duty. Hold on–Sergeant is coming with mail call!

Damn! No letter again, YOU BETTER BE SAFE. I LOVE YOU AND REQUIRE YOU FOR THE REST OF MY LIFE! You do understand that, right?? This "war" can't last forever, it just seems like it.
Love, Mary E.

January 16, 1991
Dear Dad,

Just received your package with the Rose Bowl tapes. I just got started listening to them when my Walkman died. Hopefully it's just the batteries, but I just changed them yesterday. Sorry I haven't been able to write much. We've been very busy to say the least. I'm on reactionary force for the next twenty-four hours. That just means I have to hang out in a different tent so incase something should happen there is a group of people ready to go. There is a lot of stuff going on, but of course it is the infamous, "I can't tell you." Wonder if Linda and Ken are on their way over as I hear more troops are coming daily.

I'm really, really beginning to hate this situation. It's hard not having any idea when this will actually start so we can departure. What happens if nothing every gets started? Sometimes when the rumors are really flying, I wonder if I'll ever see the States again. I realize I'm taking this too seriously. Seriousness is a necessity, but not to the point of being morbid.

Stars and Stripes reported we have to stay here nine months instead of the original six months to get credit for a short tour. I would hate to get shipped off to Korea the minute we get back (if ever) and be separated from Jason all over again. Seems kind of convenient for the Army to change that now that they see there is no way we will be out of here under six months.

Dad, you keep saying, "Get your job done and come home." Boy, I wish we could. Working with no end in sight makes for a low morale and not just mine. Boy, I must really be tired because I sure am whining, so enough ranting and raving.

Dad, you could have lied to me, by the way. You could have told me it was cloudy and nasty on New Year's Eve, and our wedding would have a been a weather disaster. Instead you tell me you were looking at the very same beautiful full blue moon, I saw. Ah, you add insult to injury.

Well, I guess I'd better get some sleep while I still can. That is kind of the motto of life–treat everything like it's your last. Eat chow, every time, because you never know when you won't get it. Wash clothes if you have a spare moment, you never know when you will run out of water. Sleep if you can, you won't be able to later.

Just a few more moments of whining, Dad, but did you ever notice that the fellas making a war aren't the ones over here really doing it? I'm realizing, to my dismay, life is run by a lot of guys making policies that they don't have to abide by. Sad isn't it. Might do well to walk a mile in combat boots before you commit them to the fight, huh? Or spend sometime in our lovely desert holding pattern before touting, "Let the sanctions work!" I love and miss you all, and I guess you know I feel pretty miserable right now and would really like to be home.

Love, Mary E.

January 17, 1991

My beloved husband,

I love you very very much! What a night and day to be on reactionary force! I pray so hard that you are safe. Oh darling, please be careful. Hopefully by the time you get this, the war will all ready be over. I sure wonder what you are doing right now.

Just remember, my darling, I love you, and I need you. This will be over soon now, and then we can work on being man and wife. Someday we'll tell our grandkids about Desert Storm. God be with you my beloved, God be with you!

Love, Mary E.

January 17, 1991

Dear Dad,

I have a big gripe tonight. Guess what I heard. Women aren't going war! Well, that's funny, what the hell am I? Really though, my favorite is the people who say, "Our boys over there." Better yet is, "how will that affect our men over there?" Now, I know it's been a while since I've seen a real shower, but I'm pretty sure of the "parts" I contain so, am I or am I not a woman? Yes, I am. Am I or am I not "over here?" Yes, I am. Am I or am I not packing live ammo twenty-four hours a day on this reactionary force? Yes, I am. Well, maybe I should just shave my head and call myself Marv. Ok, ok Dad, I'm calming down. I know I am not the first generation of women soldiers to feel this way and probably not the last either. At least I didn't really have to pretend to be Marv to be allowed to serve my country. Which by the way, right now doesn't feel quite the privilege it used to!

Do you remember when I was discussing what field to go into with you and Ken, and my brother thought Military Intelligence would be a little more elite than some other field? Hogwash! We are all just in one big mixing bowl of duties, missions and assignments, and we are all stuck over here in a place that seems dangerously close to being known as a war.

I'm sorry, Dad, I guess I vent a lot of frustration on you. Actually being on this reactionary guard makes for the longest time I've had to sit down for quite a few days. The next two weeks are going to be worse. So much for the showers and some semblance of order to our lives. It's been well over a week since I saw a shower and don't really expect to see one the rest of this month. It seems silly to base so much on a shower, but it seems as though it is your one

138

moment to wash away the grime of life and emerged refreshed and ready to move on.

I have to admit I really hate Army life today. Don't get me wrong, I love the U.S.A. and the thought of Hussein and his terrorists harming one American head on American soil is enough reason to be here, but hey! Let's get the show on the road! Do you remember after Grandpa died, I told you I wanted red, white and blue roses like a flag on my casket? I guess if I do die over here, you won't have to worry about that, I feel I have earned my flag.
Love, Mary E.

January 17, 1991
Dear Mom,
Yes, I'm in a war, but–I'm O.K. Hopefully by the time this letter reaches you it will all be over. I sure do love and miss you, and Grandma and Grandpa too. Mom, don't worry about me. Remember, Uncle Jim was in a war and he's a guy and had a way more dangerous job than me and he came home safe and sound.

What else can I tell you at a time like this that will ease your mind? Never in my lifetime did I expect to be in a war, but oh well and tah dah, guess where I am!

If you must worry, worry about Jason, but it wouldn't hurt to pray for us all.
Love, Mary E.

January 22, 1991
Dear Dad,
It's time for a real letter. I've been pretty busy lately, but I'll attempt to get an information packed (yet still interesting) letter off to you all. It's still pretty hard to imagine that I'm in a real war. I should think carrying live rounds and slapping that magazine in while on guard duty would bring it home, but it still seems so surreal that I'm personally in a war.

The night it kicked off was pretty spooky. I was on reactionary force and the Sergeant in Charge woke us up, just incase. Before I knew it, it was my guard shift. I pulled the shift with Fred. He was kidding me by saying, "My first night in combat and it's with a chick!" How ironic that at the same time he was on guard duty, his wife was having their first baby, a girl. He got the Red Cross message four days later. Without a doubt, he would have preferred to have been with her instead of at a guard point with me!

We spent the first part of our shift trying not to think about our situation. We talked mostly about horses. We heard over our radio SCUDs had been fired, and the whole camp was to be up on alert. We sat at our post, just listening. Listening for missiles, listening for the M-8 chemical alarm to go off, listening to a darkened camp seethe with activity.

I told Fred I was going to check on the M-8 alarm, but I really wanted to pee especially if we had to put our chemical suits on. They are a bear to get on and off! It seems in every tense moment, I have to pee something awful.

When I came back, Fred told me the call came over the radio to start taking our nerve agent pills. I didn't believe him, and as I was about to scoff at him, I heard the call myself. These are the experimental pills that are supposed to help you survive a nerve attack.

I was sure glad to get off the reactionary guard, but there was no time to rest. The day was spent packing and preparing for this mission we are on. As we worked, the radio was on, and we were listening to T.V. being broadcast over Armed Forces Radio. They interviewed one poor mom with all three of her children over here, and it just so happened to be the mom one of our Majors back at D-Main.

The next morning, the camp was again brought to 100% awake at 4:30am and had to go to MOPP level one. The combination of me sleeping so hard and the abrupt way we were brought awake, I really, really had to pee! I knew I didn't have time to hike all the way down to the latrines, so I just copped a squat next to the tent. Hey, we were pulling out of that patch of desert later that morning anyway. I just hoped no one would trip over me in the commotion.

MOPP gear is our chemical suit and level one meant wearing the pants and top. Good thing the weather was cool, because they feel like a snowsuit. The biggest problem with MOPP gear is, they can't get wet or the effectiveness is shortened. Who ever said it doesn't rain in the desert was wrong! It's been steadily raining for days. The last two weeks we haven't seen the sun. Is this the desert monsoon season?

Naturally I can't tell you anything about this mission. Let's just say, I can see bombs exploding in Kuwait-unless it is really foggy or raining, which it has been often. I don't mind being out here. There's much less confusion because it's just us, and it's quiet too.

Oh yes, we were only in MOPP for a day and a half and have temporarily stopped taking the pills. I assume that's a good sign and I'm glad since the pills make me feel odd. Since coming up here, we can't pick up Armed Forces Radio very often, so we don't get very much by the way of news. Sometimes we can pick up BBC on AM, but it fads away easily. We have do have access to MSE here (the Army's telephone system,) so we aren't shut off from the Army completely. What a relief–you know–in case something really big should happen, and we don't have CNN to tell us, ha!

I finally got the Rose Bowl cassette tapes to work. Must have been sand in the Walkman. I'm glad because, that's it for mail while we are here. If someone here goes out and about, they will take all of our letters and try to reach a mail drop. Perhaps you might eventually get this. I was hoping I'd get a letter from Jason before I left, but I didn't. It's a little unnerving not to have heard from him since New Year's Eve. It's hard to have a husband in a war, but I suppose it's hard to have a wife in a war, or a child or a parent, friend or any family. I just pray very hard for God to protect Jason and all the rest of us because that's really all one can do!

Dad, we've talk about over-grazing pastures back home, well it certainly has a different perspective over here. On our trip up here, we would see all these Bedouins grazing their sheep and goats. I was wondering, "What are those animals eating? Grains of sand? There appears to be nothing!" Once we stopped in the desert, I could see these tiny slips of grass, one about every foot or so. Now that it has rained so much, the sand has a faint green tint to it. Still, it makes perfect sense to me why we see so many dead goats and sheep lying around everywhere. I wonder too, "Where do they get their water?" There are only a few puddles and that's after weeks of rain. I can't imagine how they survive in the summer, and to top it off, the poor little animals have black hair! Just imagine what these critters would do if they got to graze on a lush Iowa pasture!

The hay business is booming over here. I would guess one in every three civilian trucks you see has hay on it. They must feed a lot of hay, because it seems every ounce of desert has pellet poop on it. Just another testament that every inch of desert is grazed. Thanks but no–and we thought our cattle had it rough when the pastures get short.

Where we were at before, there were interesting rock formations and dunes and hills. Here it is flat–flat as I've never seen before! Not a rise not a dip–just plain flat! I should take a picture so the next time some one tries to tell me Iowa is flat I can say, "Here! Now, this is flat!"

Further south the predominant livestock seemed to be the camels. Here it is sheep and goats, everywhere. You drive around and see brightly painted Mercedes trucks about the size of my duce, and they are full of goats. They remind me of the trucks the carnival workers arrive in back home during Dairy Day. You also see small half-ton pick-ups with goats or sheep packed in the back, as if they were dogs going out for a ride! I do wonder where the Arabian horses are, certainly not here!

Well, I guess that's about it for now, I'll have to read back through this and make sure I haven't made any OP SEC (operation security) violations. Hopefully by the time this arrives in Iowa, this war will be over and OP SEC won't matter. It is true, this can't last forever and there's always something good in everything, I hope. All my love to everyone.
Love, Mary E.

January 22, 1991
Hi Mom, Grandma and Grandpa,

Sure love and miss you! Mom, you be careful, no more falling on the ice! I'll have to employ a bodyguard for you. Hey, did I hear you say, "Not a bad idea, especially if he's cute?"

Grandma! You mean to tell me that you preferred to go to the library rather than watch the Rose Bowl? I guess you are off the hook since they lost. I didn't even get to hear the game on the radio. They aired the Orange Bowl instead. Yet, I stayed up nearly all night listening for scores. Finally about 6:30am, I heard they lost. I sure was disappointed.

Mom, I try to read your letters really slow to make them last longer! Your letter was the last letter I got before I left on this mission. I saved it, and I read a page every now and then so it will last longer. I sure love and miss you all.
Love, Mary E.

January 28, 1991

Dear Dad,

Another lonely night on guard duty, I can only hope my flashlight batteries hold out long enough to get this written to you tonight. It is so windy, but there is nothing for the wind to blow. No tumbleweeds, no trash, but every now and then I have to look up and check with the night vision goggles. I keep thinking there is something out there. I want to write to keep my imagination from overcoming my rationale. Two hours gone, two more to go. More wind, more blank darkness across the desert, and still two more hours to go. Earlier, the wind kept catching some stray hairs and they kept whipping across my face. My gloves are so thick and way too big. The fingers would bend backward every time I tried to grasp my hair. So, I kept shaking my head to move it away because I didn't want to unglove my hand. Simply taking off a glove is quite a process while wearing a field jacket, flak vest, glove liners, and holding an M-16. I must have looked like I was having a seizure, twitching and jerking at my post. I finally gave up, took my glove off and smoothed my errant strands behind my ear. With my glove off, I decided to write until either my hand freezes or my light burns out. My hair will just have to blow until tomorrow.

Actually, it is tomorrow. I have strapped my watch to my flak vest. It is too hard to read. Heck, it's too hard to even find on my wrist. Two hours and five minutes down, leaving only one hour and 55 minutes left. Guard duty with another soldier was bad enough, but now since we have moved out in the desert by ourselves on this latest mission, there are so few of us we have duty alone and it is miserable. At least it is for shorter sessions.

You would be surprised at all the things you come up with to keep your mind active. I have already thought, word for word, every song I sang as a solo during high school. I mentally went over every flag routine I have ever done in marching band. I'll admit I was tempted to use the M-16 as a flag. I'm not sure which stopped me, the thought of how ridiculous it would look, the impropriety and derelict of duty, or just my inability to move in all these layers. So, I moved on to going over cheerleading routines, especially the school song. I was even going over the famous quotes you taught me while we were in the truck delivering bulls. "Who said, 'These are the times that try men's souls'." "Hmm…let's see…Thomas Paine!" "Excellent!"

Well now, one hour and fifty minutes left. I was hoping that writing home would make the time fly by, but it doesn't.

I have gone over several scenarios to better prepare myself if something should happen while I am on watch. Imagine a man low crawling through the desert until he is flush with the burm surrounding our camp. In the shade cast by the moon, he stealthily creeps toward me. I, like Clint Eastwood, would sense impending danger. My keen ears picking up his footsteps. Just as he tries to strangle me, I reach for my pistol belt and grab my bayonet and stab him in the stomach, twist and shove the bayonet up into his ribs. He falls to the ground at my feet and I am the hero of the camp. Yes, I can hear you laughing. All my keen ears can seem to hear is the wind blowing and blowing. Besides, with all the gear I have on it would be impossible to move that quickly, let alone perform hand-to-hand combat. I feel like I did when Mom used to dress me in my snowsuit. I really wanted to play in the snow, but I couldn't move.

Naturally, the obvious choice for self-defense would be my M-16, but the ammunition is back in the tent with a metal band strapped around it. Makes a weapon seem a little less effective, doesn't it? Yes, that is just one more of the limitations set upon us. Isn't this supposed to be war where anything goes? No, not true. Can't fire unless fired upon. That makes sense because you can't lock and load your weapon anyway. Can't affix bayonets, but you can stand helpless four hours at a crack...just in case. Reality certainly isn't like the picture painted during basic training.

Two hours and thirty-eight minutes have passed, leaving one hour and twenty-two minutes to go. Dad, I believe the wind is picking up. I think it is getting even colder too. What a trick the desert has played on me. Remember when you told me to pack my long underwear? Like a silly child, I shrugged you off and thought there was no way I was going to need long johns in the desert. How quickly I regretted that decision.

Well, time to walk the perimeter. At least when I walk the perimeter it seems to get my blood flowing again. Of course, it may take up 30 minutes of my time just trying to get my glove back on my freezing fingers. If all goes well, I will return to you.

All is well, here I am. Three down, one to go. Home free now. Maybe the relief will be early, but probably on time, even more likely late, especially if it is Bill. I'm glad I didn't ask who my relief is. I always try to be a little early. I know the great relief of being set free early, even though it adds a few more minutes to my sentence. Not everyone believes in doing unto others as you would have them do unto you. Nonetheless, I hope for an early arrival. I'm sure we all do.

It would be a lot easier on duty if there were two guards, but like I said before, there just aren't enough people to go around. We are already pulling guard twice a day on top of all the other daily tasks. Fifty-six minutes to go. It will be nice to strip down to the minimum required layers and crawl into my sleeping bag for a few hours of precious sleep. I think it is a little easier to pull the midnight shift compared to the early morning shift. Early morning is the worst because by the time the shift is over, everyone is up and there is no time to go back to sleep. At least I can hopefully sneak in two hours of sleep. Better change my thoughts here, too early to think about sleeping with forty-three minutes left.

I suppose somewhere, out there tonight, Jason is probably doing the same thing, but where? I wonder what you all are doing too. What are you doing? What is Mom doing right now? Is Ken's baby Robert walking yet? What would I do if something happened to Grandma? Do you think the Army would let me come home? Would they force me to stay, saying grandmothers are not immediate family? Would they? Could they understand how important she is? My mind seems to be wandering aimlessly. I know, think positive. Nothing is going to happen back home.

Boy, is it ever getting cold. I know they say it is coldest before the sunrise, but it is too early for the sun to be coming up. It scares me Dad, to think of something happening to Jason. What would it feel like if the Red Cross came to deliver a message of death? Do you suppose I would weep and wail, scream and cry? Would I be dazed and confused or shocked into silence? Does the Army even allow for mourning? Ah, I am being morbid. All is well tonight, and I will divert my thoughts to happy times. My return home. The farm. The family. Jason alive and well with me. Thirty-three minutes still left! My mind is empty.

Hey! Do you remember that song I used to drive you crazy with when I was in the fourth grade?
Land of the silver birch, home of the beaver
Where still the mighty moose wanders at will.
Blue lake and rocky shore,
I will return once more.
Boom-didy-boom-boom-boom-didy-boom-boom
Boom-boom

I can't seem to remember all of the second verse. High on a rocky cliff, I'll build a wig-wam. What is the rest of the song? Aw, what is it? All I can think of is the *boom didies* at the end. Well, I suppose by the time you get this letter, I will have either forgotten about the song or it will have come to me.

Twenty-three minutes. At any moment a guard could be here to take my place. I am trying to see a glow from a flashlight signifying someone is awake. No light. I am so tired of starring. Starring at the tent. Starring at the black desert. Even starring at a blank page waiting to be filled. I am so tired.

Thirteen minutes left. I feel so numb. Still starring. Cold. Tired. The damned incessant wind. All I hear is blowing. All I see is darkness. I wish they would hurry up! Ten minutes to go and no sign of anyone. I wish the new guard would just get out here! Nine minutes, still waiting. Eight minutes, no one. It must be Bill, I just know it! I know it would be wrong, but I am so tempted leave this post and wake him up. I know, stay, but it would be nice to go! Seven minutes, where is he? Maybe if I jump up and down all the gear I have on will rattle the ground hard enough to wake up my relief. Four minutes and all is not well. I want to go! No minutes left. Agony is taking over. He's late. Three minutes late. Agony is turning into anger. Oh great, he's not planning on showing up. Damn it, Bill, where are you? Five minutes late and anger is turning into despair. Dad, I've been forgotten. No, wait! I see a flashlight heading out this way. Yes! I'm out of here! I've got to give a quick report and then it is off to my tent, gear off but carefully placed for quick access, just in case, you know. A swan dive into my sleeping bag, zip up, a few more moments of shivering while my bag and I warm up and then sleep, glorious blessed sleep. Well, he is almost here, it is Bill, mark your watch Dad, eight minutes late. Good Night or Morning?
Love, Mary E.

January 30, 1991
Dear Jason,

Here I am sitting in good old 201. I know that must sound like something new and exciting. Actually, we did have some "excitement" last night. We got a call saying Iraqi T-55 tanks had attacked and we were right in the path except for the Marines right in front of us.

Apparently, the tanks were disorientated and accidentally crossed the border, and our Marines opened fire on them. Those chickens went running to the other side of the road on back to Kuwait. At least that is what we are being told happened. I don't know if I believe it or not. Either way, it totally pissed me off because it interrupted the best night's sleep I was going to have in a long, long time. Finally a good guard schedule, and I have to bug-out! I can't write too much, I am so tired. I am going to try and catch a catnap while I can.

OH! Wait! I forgot to tell you. A while back we passed a phone tent so I got to call home. My sister, Susan, is going to have another baby! She is due in early September. Isn't that fabulous? I am so excited for her! I wonder if Beth wants a baby brother or sister? I bet Jerry is rooting for a son. Dad says she is pretty sick right now, and she may drop out of this semester of school.

It was kind of hard to talk on the phone. First, hearing their voices made them seem even farther away, and then they kept asking questions I just couldn't answer. Mom was really worried I that I had been near the area of the scud attacks. What a loaded answer that could have been, "Why no Mom, I am way closer to Iraq than that!" Of course, I just told her, "No, they weren't near me."

Oh Damn, no nap after all. The convoy is getting ready to pull out. I hope we will head back to our sight. More later, got to go! Love, Mary E.

January 31, 1991
Dear Jason,

Well, that last letter sure went through a lot. We did convoy back to our site behind the Marines. We ate our MRE supper while we listened to a report that said the Iraqi tanks the night before really did attack. See? I told you so! We are on a lot more strict disciplines, light, sound, and guard. I was so tired from driving last night that I went to bed because I was to have guard at 3:00am. Around 11:00pm, I woke up to shouts and orders to grab your chemical gear, dress to MOPP (Mission Oriented Protection Posture) level 3 and pack up because we were bugging out. Iraqis are on their way, again.

Well, I didn't have any packing to do because I had never unpacked except my sleeping bag. It felt so strange leaving the tents and so many things behind. People were running as fast as they could, throwing stuff on a truck. We actually traveled in MOPP level 2, which is good because it is even harder to drive with my protective mask on. We beat feet for 18th Airborne. They were bugging again too. It seems so weird for us to take flight like this, but even though our sites look well armed, we are actually little ducks sitting armed with empty peashooters, while the ammo remains banded in a can.

We were at the 18th site getting lined up for the next leg of the convoy when someone yells, "GAS! GAS! GAS!" A chemical attack! Boom! We were all flying into MOPP level 4. Mask on, and I reached down to put on my gloves and they weren't in the leg pocket of my chem suit! I totally freaked! I was frantically searching the ground, my truck, everywhere, anywhere they could have dropped, but you know I can't see worth a shit with that mask on. Even with the glasses inserts, I just can't see. I just figured, that's it. I'm dead. I was sloppy and now I'll pay for it by a horrendous death. After all this, Sergeant E was right, I am a fuck up for a soldier. How could I let this happen? About this time, Sergeant E sees me standing there without my gloves on. He motioned to my hands, then he held up his gloved hands and violently shook his hands in front of my masked face. I could hear his muffled scream, "GLOVES! GLOVES!"

I just shrugged my shoulders, what else could I do? I assumed I was screwed. I'm glad I couldn't see his face. He just turned his back, I could see him shake his head. I'm sure he was saying, "See! You stupid-ass bitch! I told you all along!" Luck was with me. It was a false alarm. I tell you, that was an incredibly valuable lesson. I finally found my gloves behind the seat in that little crack between the tarp. I have no idea how they got out of my pocket, but I'll be checking for them every chance I get. So, here I am waiting again in 201. Convoy is moving, Bye!
Love, Mary E.

February 2, 1991–I think–I do know it is Saturday
Dear Jason,

Do you remember when we were getting ready to deploy and I went to the pharmacy and got a six-month supply of the pill? The guy dispensing the medications rudely informed me, "You won't need these where you are going." To which I curtly replied, "There are more reasons than sex to take the pill!" Well, this is one of them. I have no clue what the date is, but the pill tells me it is Saturday! HA!

I sure didn't have a chance to finish that letter. As soon as we got back to our site, I had guard duty, and then we bugged out again. OK, I'll back track and try to finish the last bugging out. After the gas incident, which will be embedded in my mind forever, we drove across the desert. It seemed like we drove forever. We got to a stopping point. I would love to ask how they know when we are at a stopping point. It's just the middle of the desert to me. What makes this bit of sand more stoppable than a mile more or less?

I was able to catch a little sleep around 5:00am, but by 8:00am we were back on the road to our site. On the way back, 202 sheared off three of the four bolts that connect the steering column to drive train on the axle. I hooked my good old 201 to it and was towing it back at a crawl to our site, but I hit a bump too hard and the steering wheel locked to the left. We had to leave it there in the middle of nowhere. Once we got back to our site, some of the guys went back and had to literally drag it to 18th's site.

Meanwhile, we were checking for compromises, straitening decoys, and fixing anything that looked out of place. Then, I was off to guard duty. When I got off guard duty, I asked if I could make us a T-ration on the potbelly. I got the go ahead and I was so glad, because I really couldn't remember the last time I ate, let alone ate something hot!

I was going to sit down and write to you, but I had to go back on guard duty since Fred was still off with 202. What a light show I saw on guard duty. On top of all the flares we have been seeing the last couple of nights, it was the most extreme bombing I have seen so far. There was ARC bombing, MRLS, and you could even see tracers with the NVGs. It was kind of cool to watch, but then I realized those aren't little sparks from a fire, they are rockets aimed on a mission, and that mission is ultimate and destructive.

This time it was real. Not like the night the Sergeant W and I were totally freaked out by the huge glow on the horizon. We were watching with the NVGs until we could start seeing it with our eyes. We were trying to figure out if it was bombing or fire perhaps, when we realized it was the moonrise! Boy, did we get a good laugh on that one! But I couldn't laugh now.

I had been off guard duty for about ten minutes when the call to bug out came again. Once again, in an all too familiar fashion, we tossed our bags and got ready to roll. It was a tighter fit since we were short a vehicle. I was glad to relinquish driving duties after the initial assembly at 18th. After all the previous nights driving and all that guard duty, it didn't hurt my feelings at all. I just tucked myself between two duffle bags and held on for the ride.

Somewhere in the night, 203 blew its head gasket and oil was spewing everywhere. It is black now instead of sand color. That was the last straw. It was decided we should tear down our site, stay with 18^{th,} try to recuperate some vehicles, and then head back to our own Cav country. 201 and I pulled 203 back to 18th's site and we off loaded everything that was on the truck. Part of us went back to our lonely old sight and tore down and loaded what would fit, while those of us left at 18th loaded things on to the broken trucks. It took two trips back to get everything.

As we packed and stuffed the broken trucks, we all commented that it was strange the people from the 18th hadn't come back yet. I have to admit, in their absence we pilfered their mess tent. We have been on MREs too long and they had real food! They had some potatoes, real ones, not canned, not dehydrated but the real kind you can peel! I took out my Gerber knife and ate one right then and there. I have never tasted such a wonderful raw potato in my life! I hope it isn't stealing because I grabbed a couple more and stuck them in my bag for later. Who knows when we will eat again?

As I was heading back to the trucks, I passed a trash point and noticed a can of boot polish in there. On a whim, I stopped, picked it out, and opened it to see if there was any left in it. I felt like a bag lady rifling through trash, but my boots haven't had any polish in about two months. There was some left in that can, enough for one boot, so I dug deeper and found another can in there. It too had just enough for the other boot. Boy, I can't imagine anyone throwing this away. How wasteful. Apparently, they've seen supply more often than we have.

By the time they came back with 201 the last time, two fuel injection lines had broken. It was still drivable but max speed was 30 mph without any tow loads. We shifted loads and did a little more packing. Meanwhile, we were still wondering why no one else was here and where were they?

Around 5:30pm, some 18th guys came back for some supplies and were very surprised to see us waiting. It turns out, we weren't supposed to be in that sector all day. The sergeant informing us of this wasn't the most pleasant of people. He starts shouting at us to get out! Only he and his four soldiers have the authority to be on this site. Get out now! Well, we'd been there all day, what was the big rush? Wasn't it 18th's responsibility to inform us in the first place of the change of plans? The last word they gave us was to rendezvous at this site for mech help. Bill and Dave thought the only reason they were so hot for us to get out was so they could steal what they wanted and blame us. Made me feel a little guilty about the potatoes, but it wasn't someone's personal property, and I am very sure the polish was someone else's trash.

So, off we limped into the desert away from the 18th site and toward the 101st, hoping they would take us in for the night, a caravan of homeless vagabonds. We spent the night at 101st, but they couldn't give us any help. We had no choice but to continued on our sorry way toward Log Base Alpha. Finally 203 just couldn't go on, 201 and I kept going until we reached the Log Base. I dropped our trailer and went back for 203. 202 was actually towing it very very slowly along the side of the road, but it was very precarious because who knows if and when the drive shaft would sheer completely or lock up again. Well, while I was gone dropping off the trailer, 202 did just that. It locked and violently veered, which also sheared the towing shackle clean off of 203. This left me to pull 203 and it's trailer with a chain! I guess Fred has found a tricky way to unlock 202 by pounding it just so. I don't argue with his method, because they said they would continue to limp on so I wouldn't have to tow them.

The Log Base Alpha is the home of the Alabama National Guard, and they have been so cool to us! They said it would be no problem for us to stay with them as long as we needed and they are going to help us to fix our trucks!

Because of our warm helpful welcome here, the Lieutenant wanted to go back and sign us out of 101st. I was surprised to learn he hadn't signed us out when we left, but he was afraid we would have to end up back with them if we couldn't make LBA. So, I had the privilege to drive him all the way back to 101st.

Along the way, we passed 202 and stopped to see how it was limping along. They decided if they were still on the road on our return trip, we would tow them the rest of the way. I guess I don't mind driving LT back to 101st one bit, because tonight we will have a tent to sleep in with no bugging out or even guard duty. They said we were welcome to sleep in the recreation tent. We will not only have chow, but hot chow! Best of all, I heard they have a shower tent! I can't remember the last shower I had.

So, there you have it. Here I am waiting for the lieutenant. A very good opportunity to catch up on writing to you, although I am in hopes of writing more while we are at LBA. Maybe there is even a table to write on in the rec tent, wouldn't that be something! I love you so much. I hope things are going smooth and safe for you!

Love, Mary E.

February 3, 1991
Dear Jason,
    I'll see if I can pick up where I left off yesterday. Yes, I am at a table in the Rec tent and I slept on the *floor* last night. A table and a floor, pretty cool, huh?

    Our trip back from 101st yesterday was almost a disaster! I was nearly sideswiped by a Saudi truck. It totally sheared off my mirror and sent pieces of glass flying everywhere. You know I don't have a window on the driver's side, so I was covered in glass. I only had a couple of cuts. If that's the worse that happens to me over here, that's fine. I'm just glad I didn't get smashed.

    202 had made it to Log Base Alpha, so I didn't have to do anymore towing. I just had to get myself settled in the lap of luxury. This site has a phone tent, we may be able to get mail here, and there is a T.V. in the rec tent! I have eaten hot chow, but best of all was the shower!

    There were some Red Cross kits and as soon as I could, I grabbed one and headed for the shower tent. I was so pleasantly surprised to find out when greeted by a blast of steam that these were heated showers. The warm mist was so inviting that I was almost giddy by the time I could slip under the cascading water. I felt so decadent just standing there, eyes shut, letting the water pour over me. I felt like a melting snowman as I let the water dissolve layers and layers of dirt and cold. I could envision a shell of sludge disintegrating at my feet. Sludge that flowed out beneath the pallet I stood on. Sinking into the desert sand from which it came. For the first time in such a long time, I felt light. No weapons, no mask and for one brief moment, no worries. Just the clean rejuvenating warm water trickling over my bare skin.

    When I opened my eyes, one woman was looking at me with an odd expression on her face. I was a little embarrassed but I told her, "It's been way over a month since I've seen a shower and this is the first hot one I've had in, geez, I think since I got here in October." She looked horrified. "No way!" she answered back. I nodded yes and went back to soaking with her approval. As the water ran, I thought of how a thing like this was so common at home, but here it was a luxury almost beyond compare.

I washed my hair three times. Each time scrubbing until I thought my scalp would come loose. I thought perhaps I had used well over my quota of water and reluctantly left my steamy paradise to towel off. As I put my sundries back in the bag, I noticed a razor. I grabbed it and held it up to the light as if it where a foreign object. I didn't mull over the idea very long before I dove back into the shower and shaved my legs and underarms. Now, that was real self-indulgence. I hated having to put on that same old dirty uniform. Somehow my clean hand washed underwear didn't seem clean enough to wear either. Still, I felt several pounds lighter as I walked back to the tent.

The guys had popped in a video and were watching a movie when I got back, but I was clean, fed and very, very tired. So, I went to sleep and slept like the dead without interruption.

This morning I got to call my grandparents, but I ran out of time all too soon. It was so nice to hear their voices, but I'd rather hear yours. I'll even trade out for a letter. I hope you're o.k. I think I will try and go back to the phones if I get a chance. The guy at the phone center is from 2nd AD. It was nice just to see your familiar patch. Silly, huh?

Well, I am off to see what can be done for our trucks. I will finish this later.

Love, Mary E.

P.S. The Alabama Guard is making quick work of our problems. We fixed 201 right away because that was the easiest to do. 202 is also fixed. It took a little longer to do, but it is good to go now too. 203 is giving us a little bit harder of a time. They need some part for it that they don't have here, but they radioed for it and it will come with a truck tomorrow. OH, darn! We have to stay here one more night. Can you tell how disappointed we all are?

I thought I should make use of all of the conveniences here while I can, and I went to the phone tent again. I am missing you so bad, so I thought I would do the next closest thing to you and called your family. Your brother answered. I said, "Hi, Derek! This is

Mary." He answered, "Mary? Mary McFarland?" I had to laugh, I didn't correct him. He quickly passed me off to your Dad, I assume he is acting as the official spokesman of your family?

Apparently, your aunt and cousin saw you on CNN and called your folks, and they kept watching until they saw you too. Well, I'm glad to know you are out there! Of course, I couldn't alleviate any of their fears about you because I just don't know anything. Your dad said the last letter they got from you was December 28th. They are so worried. Me, too.

He also said that Derek got into a bad hockey fight. I know hockey fights aren't uncommon in the sport, but this one was especially nasty. Your dad thought it was fueled more by an inability to express his anxiety over you than the hockey infraction. Man, I sound like some psyc textbook. He also said they tied yellow ribbons around the two trees in your front yard, and they aren't coming off until we take them off ourselves.

Your Mom did get on the phone right before my time ran out. She told me not to worry about you because she was doing enough for all of us. She says if I do run into you, I am to tell you to take care of yourself and get yourself home in one piece. Then she added the same to me and that was the end of the phone. Your mother speaks volumes of wisdom-listen to her!

The part for 203 didn't fix it. We will be forced to tow it when we pull out for D-Main at 3:00am. I better sign off and get some sleep, but not until I get a little sappy with you. I could write for pages about how much I love you, miss you, need you, want you. I keep your plastic encased drive-on rag near me when I can. At times, I open the bag and breathe deep your scent to remind me you are real. Sometime I worry you are just dream I have manufactured in the hazy moments of guard duty. It makes my chest heavy, and I ache for your touch, your kiss.

I fear that war may turn you cold or brooding, but I hope I can keep that from ever happening strictly by my intense love for you, my darling. I believe in two constants in our world. Your eternal love for me and my eternal love for you. I love you. Good Night. Sweet Dreams.

Love, Mary E.

February 5, 1991
Dear Mom, Grandma and Grandpa,

I was just browsing through the *Upper Room* devotional book you sent, Grandma. I was looking at what days I'd missed, most of January, and saw one of the days prayer focus had been *Grandparents that are far away from Grandkids*. Do we count? Is this far enough away?

I sure hope your birthday will be happy tomorrow, Grandpa. I wish I could be there to celebrate with you. Remember, you can do anything you want on your birthday. That means, you can sleep in front of the T.V. with it on for as long as you want and Grandma can't turn it off!

Thank you for the boxes! How very nice of all of you! They were perfectly timed as I was nearly out wet wipes, paper, and envelopes, and I was starving for good American cookies. Grandma, every single cookie made it in perfect shape. I received six boxes total upon our return. I have selfishly hidden your heart-shaped special recipe Valentine cookies, Grandma. I got cookies in four out of the six boxes and will gladly share my loot, but those cookies are mine! Boy are they ever good!

I am writing this letter tucked into my sleeping bag. It is still very cool. Not February Iowa cold, but cold for us just the same. We had a lot of frost on the ground this morning but I don't think our pipes will freeze. OH! Silly me, we would have to have pipes! Seriously, I am sorry to hear it happened to you. What a mess that must be.

You said there was an outbreak of chicken pox back there? Did any adults get it? Last spring, our First Sergeant got them, and he is 45! Did little Robert get them? Ken sent me a picture of him. It makes me giggle every time I look at that little nephew of mine.

No, Mom I don't have my own tent. Gee, I'd probably be scared to stay by myself. There is a war on over here. Haven't you heard? It's not so bad with just the four of us in here. Although, the lady next to me talks to herself and that can get a little confusing and unnerving.

I have been sharing my sleeping bag with my new stuffed rabbit, Charlotte. Someone sent me a catalog ages back, and I placed an order to send a present to Jason and I added this rabbit to the order for me. It seems so childish, but then there is something to be said for that. I am sure glad I ordered her. She is soft and cuddly and a good reminder of home, but most of all very unlike Army life!

As for my correspondence courses, well, the war will be over and I'll still be taking them, but I will keep plugging away and bit-by-bit I'll get that degree!

No Mom, I didn't get to see Bob Hope. I didn't even know he or the Vice President were over here until they were already gone.

I still haven't heard from Jason yet, but I sense he's o.k. Just busy and the mail system is more messed up over here than from here to home. Boy, I'd give anything for the two of us to be together in the States–anywhere. Even Texas would be fine.

Got a letter from Uncle Jim. He said he visited you, Mom, in Waco when you and Dad were stationed there. He also admitted to getting sick when Dad took him for an airplane ride. Maybe it was a good thing he wasn't in the Air Corps after all?

I'm so lucky to have you guys as my family, and I was so lucky to find Jason with his nice family. His grandma wrote to me and said, "Even though I haven't met you face-to-face, I couldn't have hand picked a better wife for my Jason." That made me feel pretty good.

Thanks again for the boxes especially the cookies! I love and miss you all so very much!

Love, Mary E.

February 7, 1991

Dear Grandma,

I just got your letter of November 27th! I also got a lot of boxes. Your cookies, Grandma, are the biggest hit! In fact, every time I get a box everyone comes to my tent and says, "Got any of Grandma McFarland's cookies?" Ever thought of going into business? My question is, how do you get them to stay so soft? Oh yes! Thank you for the candies, too. Of course I'm not like you. I don't have the will power to ration myself to one a day.

I understand you are the pheasant lady of Iowa! They must be fun to watch. I haven't seen any animal life since the rescue of the goats. While we were at our lonely little site, we had to drive the trucks around in the desert to make it appear like we were a real site, instead of a bunch of decoys. One day, we ran into this poor fellow trying to herd his goats. Naturally, we were a little suspicious, but it didn't take long for us to realize he could really use some help. He told us in broken English that these were strays that he had been trying to get back with the rest of the flock, but they were not cooperating. We decided to go ahead and load them all into our truck and drive him home. It was quite a process to lift each goat into the truck and keep them inside while rounding up the ones that were trying to scamper away. After a short time, I could see how he could feel at his wits end. We did finally manage to get them all loaded and I stayed in the back guarding the goats while Mr. Bedouin road up-front, directing the way to his home.

His home was just a tent in the middle of the desert surrounded by more goats. It sure seemed a bleak existence compared to our lush, productive farm. I lifted each wayward sheep down out of the truck. Mr. Bedouin seemed relieved to have this task complete. I was glad we could help. I sure miss animals and our farm. I'll trade my sandstorms for blizzards any day. I'd take the –40 degrees and everything just to be out of here!

Some nights I sure could use an electric blanket. It feels cold to me, especially when it frosts, but nowhere near Iowa cold. I'll still trade, though. Well, thanks again for the boxes and the toilet paper was great boon, but most of all, thanks for the cookies. You sure have a cookie club over here.

Love, Mary E.

February 7, 1991
Dear Dad,

Thank you for the boxes! I'm wearing the flannel shirt right now. It is great for nighttime! Really, thanks for everything. I sure appreciate it all. I'll go ahead and answer Linda's letter to in hopes she's there. Sure was nice to talk on the phone wish I could tell you more but…

Shoot Dad, you say it's hard to get back to sleep after your 2:30am first calf heifer check. Boy, when I have guard duty at those hours I never have trouble going back to sleep. It's the getting up for guard duty that's tough! Sorry to hear you have lost a calf, what rotten luck. So, it's almost the 8th, I wonder if Stoney has had her calf by now. I hope you won't have any more cases of pneumonia, especially with the cold cold weather.

By the way, what is Linda's Field Hospital Number? I saw #32 and #22 over here so far. I'm sorry this is so short, but since returning from our mission, we've been working very hard on recovery, which means fixing all the things we broke. Mail is sky high, what a nice feeling!

Thanks again for the boxes. I sure do appreciate them!
Love, Mary E.

February 7, 1991
Dear Mom,

I just got a letter from you. Just to put your mind at ease, when we qualify with our weapons, we have to qualify with our chemical masks on. You can feel safe because in that part of qualification I shot 100%, a perfect shot. To be honest, it's the night time firing I have trouble with, but since I do a lot of driving that shouldn't be a problem.

Wow, what a sister I have! I can't believe that while Susan is pregnant, she is on the Dean's List! I bet little Beth is growing so fast! Does she want a brother or a sister?

I noticed you've been putting your stamps upside down on your envelopes, Mom. I can't believe you remember me saying that means I love you. By the way, I love you too. I would write MPS Free upside down, if I thought the mail wouldn't be confused, but you have to know how much I love and miss my Mom!
Love, Mary E.

February 11, 1991
Dear Family,

Please share this letter as it is all I will have time I have to write for now. Yes, I could hear you screaming all the way over here– Write! Write! Write! Just remember now, war is pretty hectic!

Found out an interesting fact yesterday. Tanks can back up. I didn't know they had reverse, but then I hadn't ever really contemplated the gears on a tank before either! Learn something new everyday, huh?

I am so amazed by all the letters I've been receiving! Overwhelming, absolutely overwhelming. That's what is really great about America. You have the ability to express yourself–positive or negative. I'm really touched that all those people took the time to write me! It's one thing to hear of the support back home from family and friends that know, love, and care about you enough to lend their support through anything, but it really makes the point when people you don't even know tell you! Incredible!

Well, let me try and to bring you up to date. Let's see, the mission. I called that place our lonely site, because it seemed to be literally in the middle of nowhere. It was pretty desolate and we sure didn't have much, very little in the way of supplies, water or support. Besides a lot of guard duty there were just a few times that stand out in my mind.

One day, Bill was on guard duty when he started whooping and hollering. We all came pouring out to see what was up, when we saw a small ¼ ton pick-up truck trying to breach our entry point. All ten of us flew into action. We had to look like a realistically manned site. We got them back in the truck and on their way. Fred and Sergeant E personally escorted them away. I am pretty sure they were Iraqis sent to check out the validity of our site. Closest we came to breaking our bands on our ammo cans.

Then, I got sick for a couple of days. We have all taken our turns with illness. I just don't think my person can go that many consecutive days without sleep, on cold, windy guard, and one meal a day without it taking a toll on the body. I lost my voice at first and had a cough. Then I started running a pretty good fever. That is when the sergeants decided to take me to a site with a medical tent. I think my little episode with the asthma worried them. I just hate being considered a weak link, but I didn't argue. I felt pretty crappy. My throat was pretty sore and my glands were pretty swollen. We had to drive about seventy-five miles one way, and when we got there they told us sick call was closed.

I've never seen Sergeant T lose his temper, but he sure got close. He informed them of our situation and a medic came over. My glands were so swollen he asked if I was chewing gum. I opened my mouth to show him, empty. He thought perhaps the doctor should come and see me, but he wouldn't get up off his cot! So, the medic relayed information by shouting answers to the doctor's questions across the tent. I was feeling a little disgusted by the whole affair. Wasn't I worth getting up for? Apparently not. The doctor just hollered back, "Give her a cold packet. I'm sure it's a virus that we can't do anything about anyway." The medic sheepishly handed me the packet made up for cold relief, and I believe his eyes were apologizing for such apathetic treatment. Sergeant T ranted and raved the whole way back to our truck about such shoddy treatment. I've never seen him do that, ever! Off we went our seventy-five miles home over the bumpy desert. I did feel better by the time we got back, and I started coughing stuff up. I'm guessing all the shaking in the truck jarred loose whatever ailed me.

The last few days at our lonely sight were pretty sleepless. Every night we were seeing flares everywhere, and we had to be ultra alert on guard duty. It was taxing before, but the stress of a known threat so near made me feel like I was constantly on pins and needles. It was hard to find anytime to sleep, and if I did it wasn't a very sound sleep. Then, it seemed every time I did finally doze off, we would have to jump up and "bug-out." You see, in Battlefield Deception if we do our job right, it's dangerous. The ten of us don't have any weapons but our M-16s, but we appear to be a whole site of about 50-60 people surrounded by M1-A1 tanks! Tell me, which do you think has an advantage: a) Soviet made T-62 tanks with a 115mm gun manned by psychotic Iraqi soldiers or b) a 2 ½ ton truck with a few incredibly brilliant and brave, yet ill equipped people with unloaded peashooters (5.56mm) in the back. Yeah, that's what we think too so, we "bug-out."

It was really weird leaving everything behind. Our tents, cots, basically all non-essential equipment. The first night after the radio sounded the alert that Iraqis were assembling on the border, which was about as far away from town to the farm, the Lieutenant rallied us. He told us if we were over run we were to scatter into the desert and lay as flat as possible since there isn't a bit of cover. The thought of doing that really un-nerved me. Just seems like there would be a better solution than that, but mercifully the word came to move and we beat feet.

Man, my eyes got so tired by driving in blackout drive. Blackout drive consists of driving by the light of a small headlight about the size of a quarter. Of course, in a convoy we look for the taillights of the vehicle ahead. They consist of four pairs of red lights about the size of those Halloween candy corns. I think they look like the face of a little devil. I am amazed we have never crashed, yet. We spent the night at a rally point in the middle of the desert. This is one time being short was handy, as I could lay down on the truck seat with both doors shut. I didn't get much sleep, but at least it was a position other than hunched over the wheel peering into the darkness ahead of me, looking for the face for the devil.

Close to dawn, we got the "all-clear" and headed back to the site and continued the mission. We didn't want to compromise the site if they hadn't penetrated into the interior. We turned east at the second sand bagged dead goat and headed to our lonely home. Just to let you know, dead goats are about the only landmarks around out here. We have posted sandbags along side certain dead goats to help mark our trails.

Dave decided we needed a new slogan and came up with, "when in doubt, we bug-out!" We were laughing hysterically, even though it wasn't all that funny, but we just had to lighten up. We were all feeling the weight of stress. We had to "bug-out" the two next nights as well before they pulled us out.

One by one our deuces have been crumbling during our night flights across the desert. Our poor 1966 vintage trucks just can't seem to keep themselves together. 203 was spewing oil everywhere like Old Faithful spews water. 202 was having some major steering problems, and my poor old 201 broke some fuel lines. As we packed up and left heading back to Cav country, our convoy had a distinct limp to it. I was even pulling vehicles with a chain! Boy, I'm glad I lived on a farm. Pulling tractors, driving trucks and hauling livestock trailers has literally become life-saving tasks.

When we reached the hard ball (paved road), I have to say there were quite a few double takes as people passed our procession only to find a GIRL in the driver's seat. I guess I don't give credence to the myth "Women drivers–No survivors!"

When we finally reached the Log (logistics) point, our vacation began! I have to say the Alabama National Guard has been the nicest, most hard working group I've seen in a long time. Truly a blessed sight for sore eyes! They have really gone out of their way to help us. I would imagine we looked pretty pitiful to them as well.

They fed us hot chow and not a single bite of it came from a pouch or little tiny soup can. I actually ate something besides cheese and crackers, but that wasn't the best part! Showers! They not only had showers, but HOT showers! The Guard let us use a large tent so we wouldn't have to off load our stuff and when I finally put the truck to bed, I made my way over to join the rest. I noticed a distinct difference in the appearance of my fellow weary travelers. Sergeants K & W were CLEAN!

I wasted no time high tailing to the shower tent. After washing in my little Tupperware bowl for well over a month and a half, that shower was absolutely wonderful.

Being clean and well fed, it did not take long for me to fall asleep on the floor of the tent. Yes, they had a floor. Sleep, uninterrupted lengthy sleep, another luxury of war.

We didn't have too much trouble fixing 201 and 202 the next day but, because of 203, we had to stay another day. No one argued. Besides a happy belly, we were really in for a treat. They had a TV! We watched a little CNN to find out what we were doing (ha) and a VCR movie. It was some really crappy movie, but I really didn't care.

Finally, we decided there was no temporary solution to 203 and we towed it with us. It really needs to go to the "Great Army Bone Yard," but we can't spare it. So, here we are back a Division Main (D-Main). It isn't the Alabama National Guard Site, but it is nice to be somewhere you don't have to worry, too much, about picking up and leaving in the middle of the night.

We have started building bunker #1,000. This one will just be known as #1,000. It's hard to leave behind the ones you name! #1 was Happy Harry's Hideaway. #2 was Black Bart's Bandit Bunker. #3 was by far the hardest to build, but the nicest after it was finished, and we called in the Rock Palace. I believe George even took up sleeping in there. It was the one and only place the wind didn't howl. Even though I know a bunker is just a bunker, I suppose we should name this one too. We certainly wouldn't want to become apathetic about our bunkers. I am kidding, you know.

We've been training for a mission coming up, which of course I can't tell you a thing about, but safe to say, I needed to write now. I just never know when I will get another chance. Oh, and Dad, the cooks tried to feed us something called a steak last night. I know you don't like us to denigrate steak with ketchup, but I just had to. To be honest, I don't know what kind of steak it was supposed to be, but it certainly wasn't Iowa corn-fed beef. Camel, perhaps? I love you all and miss you to my toes.

Love, Mary E.

February 13, 1991

MOM! MOM! A HUGE MOUSE JUST WENT CRAWLING BY LIKE HE WAS OUT FOR A SUNDAY STROLL! (Wonder where he is now?) Now, I'm all jumpy and keep looking around. I'm not scared of a desert mouse, it's just I have enough roommates already, thank you. Been pretty hectic lately. Just wanted to let you know how much I appreciate your letters. Just like a mom, you can always count on them when you need them most! I miss you heap-o-las! Let's keep praying hard and soon this may be over. Keep writing, but Mom, don't watch too much news. I don't want you worrying yourself sick. I'll be o.k. Remember, I'm a girl. I guess that's all for now, not much to tell tonight except for our unexpected house mouse, I mean, tent mouse.

Love, Mary E.

February 16, 1991
Dear Dad,

I saw Iraq yesterday–you know, it doesn't look any different from Saudi Arabia, to me. It's too bad that one man can control a *land* so brutally and cruel and then decides to violently acquire more *land* to suit his blood thirst. Borders or no, it all looks the same to him, right? All the while, the poor *land* and those upon it have to take the punishment. Enough philosophy- I'm not very good at it.

Let me tell you about my new tent mate! Bonkers, the desert rat. We named him Bonkers, because every time Sergeant W sees him, she goes, you guessed it, Bonkers! I've never seen anyone, except on TV jump up on something to get away from a mouse! I think he's kind of cute, now that I've come to know him. I'm not too excited about another roommate, but he's small and doesn't take up much space. Best of all, he's quiet, until Sergeant W sees him! He mostly comes out at night, so who could ask for a better tent mate–as long as he doesn't invade my space.

Finally for tonight, have you ever seen desert gourd? I couldn't figure out what they were for longest time, but gourds grow out of nowhere, or so it seems. There are about ten to twenty in a patch, and they are about the size of a baseball up to softball. Do you suppose that is what the goats are eating when they appear to be grazing on the sand? Well, that's all for today. I'm sending love and kisses.

Love, Mary E.

February 17,1991
Dear Jason,

Been on a mission and back. It was pretty damn scary, I'll admit to that. Bad news, I lost my Gerber knife. I had it on a 550 cord, but it must have come loose after I had to use it last night. I feel so bad and so lost without it!

While we were heading back from Iraq, all I could think of was you. I sure love you my wonderfully brave and gorgeously handsome husband. You know, you are and always will be my knight in shining armor. You rode in on your white stallion and rescued me from the dregs of a lonely existence. I love you very much, so let's go slay our nasty dragon and get on home!

I'm ready to return to the kingdom of snuggling, bubble baths and romance. All my love and I'm sending kisses hope they find their target!

Love, Mary E.

February 17,1991
Dear Dad,

OK! No more nice letters! I'm grumpy, grumpy, grumpy! The wind has been blowing furiously for the last two days, no, not a breeze, WIND! Another shmall, at least the something good in everything is wind = no flies or no wind = equals flies. Take your pick.

I'm still grumpy! Last two nights I've spent in a truck in the desert because we were very lost! Not once, but twice! That's what happens when it gets dark in the desert. Unless you are driving on the "hard ball," you can't use the headlights. You have to use black out drive. Remember that is like trying to drive with a headlight that shines about as brightly as a burned out flashlight and the taillights look like glowing red angry eyes on the face of the devil. That's where the night vision goggles come into play. Still, in the desert with no landmarks…well, if you plan to stay out after dark, ALWAYS take your sleeping bag.

The first night should be named, *The Night of the Tank Traps.* A simple principal. Dig a hole in the desert as an obstacle or "trap." At one time, we had these six-foot holes in front, back and both sides. Makes me wonder how we got there in the first place! One wheel was in a hole and Dave thought we were just stuck so he was going to lock the hubs for four-wheel drive. He got out of the truck and dropped out of sight! Luckily he was not hurt. Sand is pretty soft to fall on–even six feet down. Thank goodness he hadn't driven the truck off the edge and into it. A few inches to the left and we would have been splat. That was our worst episode but the traps seem to materialize out of nowhere. Not that I want to defend Dave and his poor driving skills, but it is very hard to see land definition with the NVGs.

We ran into some British guys that were lost like us, but they were "camping out" waiting for first light, which I thought sounded like a good idea! Aaron thought they were French and said, "They speak pretty good English." We all had a good laugh. The Brits, with their thick French accents (ha), asked us to stay with them for the night, but to my dismay, my superiors chose to keep fording on.

After a few more near misses with more tank traps, they finally admitted that we should probably stop before we got farther off course. We just sat there in the truck, and waited for first light. We pretend to try and get comfortable, but it was cramped, stuffy and unnerving. As I tried to will myself to sleep, I thought of those British soldiers and wished we could have stayed there. At least there would have been safety in numbers.

The second night getting "re-lost" was much less eventful. There was one glaring exception. Dave hit a HUGE bump, which sent us flying everywhere. I swear he is the worst driver! I landed on the floor of the backseat, weapons falling in on top of me. My glasses were nowhere to found. Finally, Fred found them by his feet, in the front seat! We all insisted–Dave! SLOW DOWN!

Now, I'm back in my tent and grumpy. There is no hot chow for lunch. Mail is screwed up, again. The tent is about fall from all the wind but…I got my laundry back-and only thirteen days after turning it in! I had been given a laundry bag full of clothes from a soldier name Slause. The people at the laundry truck asked me, "Are you sure it isn't yours?" "Well, first of all, my name is S-T-A-B-E not S-L-A-U-S-E and second, I don't wear briefs!" I guess it was number two that really convinced them. They finally found and returned mine today. Believe it or not, nothing was missing!

Well, I don't feel quite as grumpy anymore, and I think the wind may actually be dying down-maybe. Perhaps it's just wishful thinking, no, wait a second-no it must be dying down, a fly just flew between my nose and this letter.
Love, Mary E.

February 18, 1991
Dear Jason,

Guess what! I unrolled my sleeping bag last night, and what was there? The Gerber! I'm so happy I didn't lose it after all. I borrowed George's stone and sharpened it, but, of course, not as well as you would have done. Just another thing, Darling, you do so very well for me. It's the simple things like a nice sharp knife that open my eyes to just how much I depend on you.

I sure had a scare last night. Someone told me a Bradley and a GSR team had been shot by the friendly fire of an Apache. My heart stopped. What little reason I could muster was the only thing that prevented me from being in an instant state of hysteria. I took in a breath and asked, "Was it a track?" "Yes!" I breathed out, but with a heavy sigh mixed with relief and sorrow. Sorrow for the families that have lost their loved ones, but great relief that you are still safe, or so I assume. I live on the no news is good news principle. Until the Red Cross starts looking for me, I will assume you are fine.

I had a good day in Saudi terms. I took a hot shower, ate a hamburger, and went to a PX that didn't have a two-mile long line. They actually had Heresy bars and wet wipes left in inventory. It was nice to get away from duties and missions, if just for a little bit of time. I Naturally, I would prefer to nibble your ear than a candy bar, but I guess we have to take the best we get.

I know this goes without saying, but I am really getting tired of this war and especially of our separation. Please know that my love for you grows stronger and stronger every day, hour, minute.

When we get home, will you do me a favor? Will you itch my back? I'll pay you back, I promise, it'll be your choice. I love you so very much!

Love, Mary E.

P.S. I can't sleep worth shit tonight so I guess I will add to this letter. I bet you are so tired by now. I'm sure you are doing mission after mission nightly by now. I wish there was some way I could help you, but I know we each have our own integral duties to do.

I think I have a bellyache from the candy bar today, or maybe it is just the continual ache I feel because I miss you so tremendously bad. Please, please be safe sweetheart. The closer the threat of a ground war gets the more I worry about you. I hope you can stop to eat at least once a day. You were too skinny when we left, I hope you get some food and water isn't too short. I know I'm rambling here, but isn't it my job as your wife to take care of you? I can't think of any other way to do that right now. I certainly would prefer to do in person, but paper is all we have for now.

Oh, why doesn't that idiot just pull out of Kuwait so we can all go home? I can't imagine how hard you must be pushing yourself right now. I sure wish you weren't with the Marines. It's oh-so dangerous! Well, I better try again to get some sleep. I too have a

busy day ahead tomorrow. I do want to tell you that no matter what happens to me, please remember I love you with my whole entire heart, body, mind and soul. I know we haven't been married very long, but you have made me the happiest person in the universe. Thank you, my darling.
Love, Mary E.

February 20, 1991
Dear Jason,
I am on cloud nine after receiving a letter from you today! Oh, I'm so happy! It is our anniversary of ten months and God saw fit to let me hear from you! I know what you mean, I always dream about you too, when I get to sleep. I think about you always. Last night I really needed one of your special hugs. You know how much I hate thunder? Well, I hate artillery even worse.

I think back to our time in Tent City, and how much I would give just to be back there. Even if I couldn't be with you, I would savor seeing you once a day and delight in stolen kisses on the way back from the latrine.

It's weird how we both know better than to worry about each other, but our hearts do it anyway. I'm glad you love me enough to worry about me, thank you. I wish you were taking care of me, too. I love being your wife, and I love you!

As much as I enjoyed your letter, I still have so many unanswered questions. What are you doing? Where are you doing it? Are you still with the Marines? Are you working too hard? There were some Long-Range Surveillance guys here for a while. It gives me hope that you can get "back" somewhere to eat and sleep for a bit.

Here is a compliment for you. When I got your letter, Davy said, "You must really love Jason to death, because every time you talk about him your eyes flame up and your face gets about as bright as the sun. I hope some day I'll meet someone that will love me as much as you do Jason. Hell, a quarter of it would do me!"

I guess when someone loves somebody as much as I love you it is impossible to hide. Nicest part is, I don't want to hide it, I want to broadcast it to anyone and everyone that will listen. "Now hear this! Now hear this! I am damn proud to be Mrs. Jason T. Stabe!" Stay safe, husband.
Love, Mary E.

February 20, 1991
Dear Emily,

I was so pleased to receive the letters you and your class wrote to Jason and me! I really appreciate that you write to Jason, I know he really likes to get your letters. I haven't seen him since Christmas. I really miss him, but then, I really miss you too!

I hope you are studying hard in school and not chasing the boys! I don't want to hear any reports of my little sister chasing boys! Are you going skiing next month? I sure wish I could go with you.

Thanks again for writing me! I will try my best to answer all of your classmates!

Love, Mary E.

February 20, 1991
Dear Susan,

I wanted to write to you because I hope you will understand. I always feel I need to shield Mom from some of the stuff that happens over here. On the other hand, I feel like I have to put on a brave face for Dad. After all, I am a soldier. My heart is heavy tonight, so very, very heavy, and so I turn to my sister. This seemingly endless waiting game is really taking a toll on my nerves. Ground war or no ground war. I've been on every detail you can think of. Sometimes I think the NCOs get some sort of sick pleasure from seeing how many details one enlisted soldier can be on in one day.

My main relief lately has been writing home and answering any soldier mail. Maybe it's some sort of strange ego trip for me, but it is refreshing to read those any soldier letters. Most of the letters I have picked up before have been from adoring school children. You know, class projects or extra credit. That is until tonight. My letter tonight read:

Dear Soldier,

How do you feel to be fighting over oil? How awful you must feel taking over those poor people's country trying to save it for us. How do you feel getting ready to kill innocent people? How can you live with yourself?

I gazed in disbelief at the letter, while tears began to fall down my cheeks. All I could think of were the young children that have flocked around my truck calling "Eat! Eat!" Think about the young women, maybe the same age as me, as you, whose lives have been shattered by rape, torture and murder. This war is over way more than oil. This is over more than simply the comfort of the U.S.

How can I be expected to answer questions like that? How can I make them understand the realities I have seen over here? I cried, Susan, hard, gut-wrenching sobs. I thought that I must have finally reached the point of no return.

Thankfully, no one else was in the tent at the time. I didn't have to explain myself to anyone. I think I have pulled myself together again, but my heart is heavy and tired. So very, very tired. Thanks for your help, I'm heading to bed. Who knows what tomorrow will bring?

Love, Mary E.

February 21, 1991
Dear Dad,

Here is a roll of film for you to develop. I hope you won't regret sending me a camera. No promises on the quality of the picture taking. Most of the pictures were taken out of my duce window, and while I was driving at that!

I hope Grandma's blood pressure is coming down. I hope I am not part of the cause of such high blood pressure! What is the latest on Linda? Will she be coming? Does she even know?

Dad, our W-2s should be coming to you at the end of this month, but you won't have to do our taxes. As long as we write DESERT STORM across the top, we have an automatic extension. Thanks for your help on that kind of stuff.

Well, I'd like to gently make birthday present requests. Mind you, no one is obligated to send anything, but I figure if you plan on it, you should at least have some idea of what to send, right?

Mary's birthday list:
WD-40
A knife sharpener
Wet wipes
Music tapes
And from Grandma (only if her blood pressure is back down!) Cookies!

I finally managed to send in a correspondence course assignment for my new class. I'm not sure if it was wise or not to be taking *Suffering, Death and Faith* during Desert Storm! Not only am I very busy, I can't seem to read too much at a time. My

mind seems to wander onto deeper thoughts about what the book is discussing and I forget to keep reading. I know, I know, it's nothing new for my mind to wander. Take care back there!
Love, Mary E.

February 23, 1991
Dear Dad,

We have watched (or I should say listened) to another deadline come and go. Everyone in the tent is trying to "carry on", but the radio is on and no one is moving, let alone talking.

Which is the worst or best of two evils? Ground war or no ground war? No one wants to die, but if a ground war is the next step of our mission, then that's our path.

Listening, listening and for the first time I believe the soldiers know more than the radio. We know when the ground war will start and we wish we didn't!

Dad, sorry this is short. The ground war has my attention. Sometimes I am so worried, I'm just not ready to be a widow. I hate knowing just how dangerous Jason's job is. I can't tell you how much I wish there was a non-violent solution to all of this, but that decision wasn't in our hands. Pray for us, pray for us all.
Love, Mary E.

February 23, 1990
Dear Me,

This is no doubt a terrible Operations Security Violation to write this letter to myself, not that it will ever be sent anywhere, but yet I am putting pen to paper. Seems pretty silly to write myself a letter, but I don't know what else to do right now. I have no one to talk to. My tent mates are nice enough, but they are NCOs. I sure as hell can't really talk to the guys! I can't tell Jason, because he will worry. I can't tell my family at home for a lot of reasons least of which is the security violations.

I have put so much time and energy into letter writing, but perhaps it would have been a good idea to keep my own journal, a Diary from the Desert. A place I could pour my heart out to without risking anyone else. Well, I will just write this letter to me for now, because I am so worried and my heart is so heavily oppressed. I must do something.

It is hard to know that the ground war will start in five hours and not be able to say a word about it. It's been hard knowing the clock was ticking on the ground war the minute we went on that last mission. Since we got back, it is hard to do anything but watch the hours tick away. So here I sit, knowing...waiting...praying for the safety of us all.

There have been so many things over here I haven't been able say anything about. It seems I have buried them into the recesses of my mind, trying to forget about them, but now those corners are overflowing.

It just isn't possible to tell your husband your Sergeant told you that if we got into a heavy combat situation he would slit my throat and leave me for the greater good of his troops. Greater good of his troops my ass! I've worked my butt off over here and you can't tell me that if push came to shove I wouldn't hang. Hell, I could probably the carry out likes of Dave. I know I've been sick a couple of times, but I'm not the only one. On the other hand, there have been times I've been so incredibly scared I thought I would puke. I just shook with fright when I felt the deep rumble of artillery reverberate inside my chest. Maybe I am a fuck up of a soldier after all. Yet, I didn't bolt, I didn't freeze. I don't know what to think.

I do know it just isn't possible tell my family that on our last mission when we asked why we weren't going into it in MOPP gear, the reply was, "Just get out there and do it! You are expendable!" Yeah, expendable like a dead battery or maybe the dirt dish water?

I can't even put on paper, let alone tell my family of the shit I've seen. The nameless bodies brutalized by a mad man. I can't do it. I have eyes, I have ears, and I have a memory that will never forget that there is more to war than oil.

I know this hasn't been any Vietnam. I have been here a little over half the time of a tour of duty in Vietnam, and I don't even want think how long tours in World War II lasted. Yet, I am here and this is real and it hasn't been a cakewalk. I am not in the rear with the gear. This is an unforgiving desert, sometimes raging hot, sometimes numbingly cold.

Too be honest, it has been a kick in the pants to actually do what I was trained to do. More so, it was a little bit of a shock it actually worked, but how can I admit that?

I hate being away from my husband, that is no secret, but more than just the separation, I hate wondering if he is still alive. I hate the nights when my mind races, imagining what I would do if the Red Cross came to tell me he was dead. Playing the scene over and over in my head until I begin to doubt what is real and what is only in my head. How can I tell anyone that I worry if I am all right? Maybe I'm losing it, maybe I'll be the next Sergeant R.

I struggle with the guilty knowledge I resent Jason. Why did he have to tell me the story about when he went to a fortuneteller? She told him in the third year of his enlistment he would be killed and guess what...war came in the third year of his enlistment. I resent Jason for volunteering to come here, a fact I didn't know until we were here. That's just fucking nuts! Yes, it has been great to see him when we did, but damn it, I wouldn't be so worried about him if I knew he was safe at home. I didn't have the luxury of choice.

And this whole woman issue is wearing very thin with me. Why is it such a big shocker to people that women, the bearers of children, go to war. It really shouldn't surprise anyone. They have been doing it since wars began. Think of Molly Pitcher in the Revolution and all those women who have disguised themselves as men, just to fight for the freedom they believed in. They have always been there. Often forgotten. Often Minimized. The "boys" over there, they say back home. No, I haven't gotten a purple heart, and I'm sure I won't get a bronze star, but I AM here. I've done my duty, and, by God, I believe I've done it damn well. More than most folks will ever be able to say.

I'm sure when it's over, people will forget, but I won't. I know it will always stir my guts. It will always make my chest ache. I hate that I had come here. I hate that my husband had to come here. I hate that anyone had to come here. I look back at those last lines and wonder what lasting effect all this will have on me. All that hate. Will I become as hardened as those responsible for us being here? Will I become no better than the enemy we are trying to overcome? I think, perhaps I should end this now and pray. Pray for my own forgiveness. Pray for safety, comfort and peace. Just Pray, because I know the storm is coming.
Love, Mary E.

February 25, 1991
Dear Jason,

We are here at D-Rear right now. We keep floating between D-Main and here. We are waiting to go on a follow-up mission, but I keep praying it will be cancelled. If it is cancelled, then I will know the reports of our brilliant success are true. If it is true, then I wonder if you aren't in Kuwait City by now. If you are, what does Kuwait City look like? I have heard the Tiger Brigade has still been moving with the Marines. Bet you have been on a ride of your life. Just as long as that life stays safe!

Drive-on, you Jarhead attachment! Let's get this over with!

Love, Mary E.

February 26, 1991

PEACE, PEACE, PEACE! WE WANT IT! WE NEED IT!

Dear Mom,

We are all glued to the radio–or should I say our headphones. They seem to be permanent fixtures on everyone's heads. We are hoping and praying to hear a bit of good news like Saddam is history, perhaps?

Support for President Bush is very high, but in our opinion our mission is not yet complete, because our righteous indignation for Hussein is even higher! How dare Hussein say he is withdrawing and telling his poor people that they are winning? How cruel can he be? Don't answer that, I already know! I've seen his handiwork.

It is nice to know people are dancing in the streets because of the USA. I am so glad to be an American. Yippee! and Hurrah! for the Liberation of Kuwait! Just imagine, Mom, your daughter is part of the successful rescue of Kuwait! A cease-fire can't be far behind this triumphant day. I'll be back safe and sound before you know it, Mom!

Love, Mary E.

February 27, 1991

Dear Jason,

I got five letters from you today. Lucky, lucky me! The radio is saying Kuwait is liberated! What outstanding news! The liberation is complete! Hoorah! Now, what do you say, on to Baghdad?

Thank you for the Valentine. Where ever did you come up with it? You and your magic bag of tricks, huh? I feel bad that all you got from me, if you got it, was a sorry drawing I made. It was sure sent with love.

I am starting to hear rumors about going home. It's hard not to get excited about the prospect. Wouldn't it be wonderful if we could be together for our first anniversary? Well, I don't want to get my hopes up too high, but that sure would be great!

I hope you will be able to read this. Our tent leaks so bad. It is hard to find a dry spot anywhere. Funny, all this rain in the desert. Damn oil fires are sure screwing with the world. I heard someone say they are getting more rain right now than they have in years combined. We have been getting quite the storms even including some thunder, lightning and high winds. Hold on to the tent, Girls, it's going to be a bumpy night! I seem to be soaking wet all the time. Makes me think of a certain night I got soaking wet in a sudden downpour with some special guy. That was quite a night, wasn't it? I can just see that precocious smile of yours.

Since everything is moving so quickly, I'm guessing it's ok to tell you a little more about this mission I was on. We knew this BIG mission was coming, and we were practicing our asses off to get right before we went up and practiced it with the Bradleys and Abrams tanks. Sergeant T pulled me aside and said the high Army officials declared I was not to go on the upcoming mission because it was penetrating too far north, but the Cav would leave it up to Bat-D to decide. In essence, they didn't want to know if I went. So, he asked me, "Do you want to go?" I answered, "Yeah, I want to go! It's my job!" He replied, "We thought you'd say that." So our team stayed as it was.

We rolled up in our trucks to the site where all the tankers were at, and part of me was a little embarrassed because there were about 300 guys that were naturally NOT expecting any women for miles around. Some were taking makeshift bathes or taking a piss or dump wherever. But the hard core part of me knew this was all in day's work, and I drove on. When I jumped down out of the truck, word spread like a rumor in a small town that there was a chick on site. They didn't have too long to ponder the oddity because the call for the practice run came. When we practiced the mission, everything worked beautifully. The smoke cover went exactly like it was supposed to and we worked flawlessly.

True to form, right before we went live and rolled, I had to pee. I grabbed my rain poncho from under the seat, jumped down out of the truck, and copped a squat next to the running board, hoping there was enough billow in the poncho to hide my parts. I didn't have enough time to worry about it because we were off and following the Bradley's. We let the engineers blow the burm and then we started deploying our tank decoys. In the end, it would appear we had penetrated into Iraq to stay. This all had to be done in under an hour. Meanwhile as we worked, we were wondering if we were going to draw fire or not in response to the friendly artillery zooming overhead.

Of course, they had to take real M-1 tanks for the tracks and sound, and in the real mission the wind changed on us. The smoke came right back on us so we were working in the cover instead of behind. I had the compass and was to heading to my point, when Aaron started screaming, "TANK! TANK! OH MY GOD TANK!" We were on a direct line to intersect with an M1 Abrams. You can just imagine who would have come out the winner of that collision! Well, I had to keep going, we were on a time limit and, damn it, the tank was in the wrong place. It was so loud I don't know if Fred and George in the back could hear me or not, but I shouted, "Hang on!" and punched down the gas. I swear I could hear them hollering, "Shit! OH! Shit! But it was hard to hear anything over Aaron's shrieks in the front seat! I had to give him such a hard time later about screaming like a little girly! He, Fred, and George all agreed I had a death wish, and was the only person in the entire United States Army willing to take on a tank! I asked them, "What was I supposed to do? I had to stay the line!" We could laugh afterward, but at the time, man, was the tension at an all time high. One slip and that could have been a serious cluster-fuck. You know, I don't suppose a single tanker ever gave "The Chick" a second thought when we started to roll.

We lost a tank to the enemy when we went to recover them two days later. I'm sure that's what happened to it. Our decoy's tracks don't really work, and it couldn't have pulled it's own stakes and driven itself off, especially since it is just a decoy image on a canvass. The generator that ran the replicating heat sensors was gone too. We set-up in the daylight, but we had to retrieve them in the cover of darkness and without any escorts. Kind of an eerie feeling to know somewhere, in the dark, there were Iraqis watching us.

We were supposed to also have a mission to replicate you! Yes, we were trying to devise a way to appear to be GSR, but with the success of the ground war that mission was scrubbed. Good thing too, because we weren't having very good luck coming up with anything believable.

Speaking of you, to be brutally honest, "This Chick" is so incredibly horny for you, I think I'm going to explode. I have missed you greatly, but it seemed with all the stress and shit going on, well, those really strong desires were kind of on a back burner. Now, well... I miss you more and more and in more and more ways! I guess I'm stuck with the same relief as you are in the form of hard labor and cold showers which is convenient because that's all there is.

We started building another bunker again. I shoveled all morning and used the pickaxe all afternoon. Tonight the guys were all whining about their blisters and I looked at my own hands. I don't have a single blister, and I know it isn't from me slacking. You'd think after all this time, they would quite being such a bunch of pansy-ass guys.

I'm glad that I can finally admit to you after all this that yes, I agree, it was exciting to really do my job. Speaking of my job, I ran into Tyler over here. His unit is "camped" nearby. He said he ran into Mark so that makes four out of the five in my A.I.T. class over here! I wonder how many of your class are over here. I suppose many of them are still in Korea and not here. Seems strange, we will all be wearing a combat patch from now on. Well, I'm damn proud. I hope you are too! I am so proud of you! I love you so much! You are an incredible person, and if I weren't married to you, I sure would be glad just to know you!
Love, Mary E.

February 28, 1991
Dear Dad,

The word is...Cease Fire! We are all hoping it is final, but we are still not counting on it. We went ahead and finished our bunker today. It is threatening to storm again. We were rushing to get all the sandbags laid before the rain hit. I could hear a generator in the background. It reminded me so much of home. I thought of how sometimes we rush to get the hay up, while the generator was Grandma furiously trying to get a little more lawn mowed before the rain. The weather started warm this morning but quickly cooled, followed by an ever-increasing breeze. The clouds were getting darker and I caught myself looking to the sky making sure there weren't any tornado clouds. Then I remembered, it was sandbags, not hay bales and I was in Saudi Arabia, not Iowa. I wonder if there are ever tornadoes here?

Anyway, it's cease-fire day, and I hope that is all I have to say for today.

Love, Mary E.

PS sorry about the canned chili-mac spots. Don't have enough paper to get you a fresh sheet.

February 28, 1991
Dear Mom,

I hope the word we are hearing about Cease Fire is for real! I keep thinking of the episode of M*A*S*H where they rumor a cease-fire, but in the end, it's still war. Since this is a real world situation, and we don't need a new episode for next week, a cease-fire would be great!

I can't wait to live in a house again. I sure would love to wear a pair of jeans, and I sure would love to eat out or do anything normal! Pizza Palace pizza sounds so good right now. I sure love and miss you. I tried to draw you a teddy bear as a card, but I'm afraid it didn't turn out to well. It's for you just the same.

Love, Mary E.

March 4, 1991
Dear Jason,

I got three letters from you today! Yippee! I sure love getting letters from you! I sure love you! Maybe if we are lucky, by the time you get this letter, we will have seen each other. I understand Tiger Brigade is coming to our neck of the woods. I sure can't wait to see you!

Yes, I'm still here at D-Rear. It is back to duty queen for me. I had KP today. I tallied up my details yesterday. So far, not counting our mission time, I have had guard duty forty-one times, KP twenty-two times and shit burning eleven times and at least thirteen police the area calls. The fun just never ends. To be quite honest, I think it sucks! I even had to peel potatoes just like on M*A*S*H!

I also had to clean the portable KP trailer ovens. The oven cleaner splashed on my nose. I tried to wash it off right away, but it still burned a little. I sure hope it is better by the time I see you. I know I will look desert worn and filthy as it is.

It's been so cloudy all day and now the wind is picking up again. I suppose it will storm again tonight, and I will spend most of it holding the center pole hoping that it doesn't come down on us.

I've got a funny little story for you. When I was in Spanish class at the University of Iowa, we always had conversation practice.

We were supposed to pick a made-up name, and I always chose Senor Pequeno, Mr. Little, because I always liked the Littles series of books as a kid. I don't know if you know who they are, but they are the little people with tails that live in the walls of the Biggs' house. Anyway, today the sergeant in charge of KP was Sergeant Pequeno. I thought that was so funny! I really did a double take at his nametag. He probably thought I was goofy in the head.

I was sure glad to hear you are keeping safe. It can't be too much longer until I see you again. The I-miss-you's are worse than ever. Everything I do makes me think of you even more than I already do, which is all the time, so it's Jason squared now.

Sweetheart, do you think it would be all right to buy a VCR when we get home? I don't want to have to leave the house anymore than we have to. We could rent a bunch of movies for a weekend and snuggle up on our bed and watch movies and eat popcorn. Oh, come on, popcorn doesn't leave crumbs in the bed. Remember how in our apartment you could move the TV on the table and see it from any room in the whole place? Yes, I suppose we could move around, but the bed just seemed a good idea so I could catch a nap during the boring parts of your gangster movies. Oh, just kidding.

I sure love getting your letters, and I am anxiously waiting to see you in person! Oh boy! Oh Boy!
Love, Mary E.

March 5,1991
Dear Jason,

Guess what? I got a letter from you today dated from January 19! It sure took a long time to get here. Do suppose it went to the states and back? I'm hiding out in our bunker today. I've found it's a great place to hang out. It is quiet, there is no dust, no wind and it is always a comfortable temperature. There is just enough room for two to live comfortably, by Army standards anyway. How about it, Baby? Come share a bunker with me?

Very good sign today, we turned in our ammo. So, I guess it can't be too long now. Seems like I keep saying that, but I guess I figure if I keep saying, one of these days I'll be right! I just miss you so much! I know it's silly to think we will never fight all of our married life, but if I ever get to complaining too much, just remind me of this experience! I bet I'll shut my trap pretty fast!
Love, Mary E.

March 5,1991

Dear Dad,

I know I write pretty sloppy as it is, but please endure this chicken scratch as I have a legitimate reason today. I had KP yesterday, and they wanted the oven and pots scrubbed with this toxic oven cleaner. It ate right through the gloves they issued me and ate my fingers raw! I even accidentally splashed a little on my nose and burned a spot on my nose raw! That was worse than battery acid! Talk about chemical warfare! So, it's pretty hard to write with tender fingers, but there is so much to tell!

Today we turned in our ammo! Yippee! No ammo! No war! I take that as a very good sign. There are some other good signs too. We were told to start making "lost" lists, which consists of stuff your section lost, or things that were stolen or destroyed. We have also started working on our vehicles again.

Jason and I might make it home for our anniversary yet! I'll give the Army Halloween, Thanksgiving, Christmas, New Year's, no church wedding, Valentine's Day, Easter AND my birthday, but please let us have our 1st anniversary together! Hope my nose heals before I see Jason again. I'm sure I look funny enough as it is!

Now, let me tell you about our trip to town. When we first arrived at this site, the town nearby seemed dead. Just a few cars, all male population and most stores were closed.

We were trying to build a wooden box to store loose decoy parts, but we couldn't come across the right kind of screws for attaching the hinges and lock. Army supply didn't seem to have any, which really shouldn't come as a shock to anyone. We decided to go to the town to see if we could find some screws.

What a transformation the cease-fire has made! People are everywhere! Flags are flying everywhere and on everything. This one truck had a huge Kuwait flag on the left and a bigger American flag on the right and a Saudi flag in the middle. I'm not exactly sure how he managed to see enough to drive!

Practically every kid we saw was waving an American flag in one hand and giving the peace sign with the other. All of them were wearing huge smiling grins. It's very gratifying to be an American.

We parked the truck to start our screw search. You know, I have been trying to learn some Arabic while, and I have become fairly efficient in numbers and some simple words, but hardware store wasn't one of those words. We found a place advertising car parts and thought we would try there.

The man welcomed us into his store very enthusiastically. We asked about screws in English, of course. I have to admit, for all my efforts to learn to read Arabic, I haven't learned a single Arabic phrase. Everyone speaks English so well!

The storekeeper said he would go get the screws we needed if we would agree to come inside and sit for a while in his store. Naturally, Aaron and Fred, in their first ever act of gallantry, eagerly offered the chair to me.

We expected the storekeeper to go in his back room for the screws, but much to our surprise, he went out the front door. After a little while, he returned. In the meantime, news was spreading that we were in the store and more and more Saudis began to flood inside.

Upon the storekeeper's return, we had to wait for their lengthy greetings consisting of three kisses on each cheek by each person! Naturally, I was excluded from this formality, but you should have seen the looks on the guys' faces as they were jerked into tight practically face-to-face conversation. We Americans just aren't accustomed to close encounters, if you will.

When we were finally given our screws, Aaron took out his wallet to pay the storekeeper said, "No Money, No Money! You're Americans!" Aaron said, "Are you sure? We really should pay for these." The whole store erupted with shouts of "No money!" so we graciously thanked them and headed out the door through an ever increasing animated crowd.

We decided to look around the town since it isn't off limits anymore. About two doors down was the hardware store. There were screws, nuts, bolts and nails all lining the front windows. I assume this is where our man had run to for the screws. I call that service! You don't get directions to the store, the store comes to you!

There were a lot of people including other soldiers out and about. Everyone is glad for a cease-fire.

As we passed one clothing store, a younger looking man came out and asked, "Picture? Please, picture in my store?" We went into his store, and out came the camera. He took a picture of all of us standing by his cash register.

Then he handed the camera to Aaron and asked, "You take picture please?" Aaron replied, "Yes." With a nod of thanks from the man, he pointed to me and said to Aaron, "Picture?" So, I stood next to him and had my picture taken. Now, I can hear you gasping, because yes, I still hate getting my picture taken, but how could I say no?

It was then I realized what a novelty I must be in town and in his store with my blonde hair and green eyes. I was instantly filled with so many conflicting feelings. Was he too shy to address me directly or was it his culture not to speak to me? I have heard stories that the Saudis believe the female troops are just here to "service" the male soldiers. Did he think he was getting his picture taken with a prostitute? Was he just pleased to have Americans in his store?

After leaving the store, I was more aware of my personal situation. I saw only one other female soldier amongst the quick moving black blobs of flowing veils and down cast eyes. These black blobs were bustling and herding children like a goat herder herds his sheep.

For one moment, I got a look at brown eyes peering out from behind all the drapery the women wear. It reminds me of a ski mask with a veil attached. I can only imagine how hot that must be in this climate. How hard must it be to simply breath.

The stores are all pretty small. They are about the size of a gas station convenience store. This is a fairly small town, so I assume the size of the stores correlate to the town size. For the most part, they consist of a long counter and aisles crammed full of stuff almost to the point of no room to walk. Makes me think of what an old mercantile must have looked like in the United States.

We went into an appliance store. Everything looked pretty much the same, except they were all a lot smaller. The refrigerators were about half the size. Now, I would have thought in this climate, refrigerators would have been bigger!

They have the cutest little washers and dryers! For starters, they are plastic. They stand about the size of a clothes hamper. Three-quarters of it is the washer side and the other quarter is the dryer side. The largest one I saw was about the size of the play by numbers organ I got for my birthday once.

I spent quite some time trying to figure out how I could get one home! They would fit perfect in a small apartment, which is why I assume they are so popular here. I realize I wouldn't be able to wash a whole set of BDUs in it, but boy it would be handy for the rest of the stuff! Funny, I am drooling over a washer and dryer like it was a pair of skis or something! Good Grief! Well, it was cute!

As we headed back to our site, the guys wanted to stop at a roadside food stand for some chicken. I declined. I didn't make it this far to be taken out by poorly prepared poultry! I did opt to buy a bag of potato chips, but the only ones available were seafood flavor. Despite my reservations, I bought them. Big mistake, BIG mistake, GROSS!

To finish out the day, we happened to drive by a P.O.W. camp. Wow, were there a lot of soldiers there. It looked more like a big get-together, like maybe the Rendezvous Day at Fort Atkinson, but it didn't strike me as looking like a P.O.W. camp except for the wire and sprinkling of guards. It was funny though, the Iraqis were using the wire as clotheslines. I wouldn't blame them one bit if they didn't want to go back!

Well, I guess that is about it. Hope you can decipher some of this. No more oven cleaner for this soldier! I think I'll stick to the potato peeling. My hands may get pruned up, but at least the skin is still there! Oh boy, the more and more people that pull into this sight, the more and more potatoes I get to peel! I'm not complaining, really!

I sure love and miss you! I know it will be soon now that we will be heading home! I just really hope all the support we've been receiving doesn't come to a screeching halt since the war has. I hope everyone keeps up such a great showing until we get home, which better be soon!

Love, Mary E.

March 9, 1991
Dear Dad,

Boy, Iowans sure do write a lot, but trust me I'm not complaining! I see now that my numerous pen pals from my younger years were just training for this flood of letters. I sit down each day and try to answer them all the same day. I never know what tomorrow will bring. Time seems to run at an odd pulse of fast and slow around here.

I believe I can safely say I have received letters from every walk of life and every part of the state! It's great, but still so overwhelming that they are all writing me! I saw the mail clerk in the chow line yesterday and he said, "There she is. The lady that gets the most mail in the Division. Heck, you practically get more mail than half the Division put together!" I told him, "I'm very proud of that fact! I'm an Iowan you know!" "Yes," he said, "I know, I know, I handle your mail, remember?"

We both laughed. Boy is it nice to laugh now and then!

Things are so much less stressful now that the war is over. It's much better now that we can resume some activities, especially PT. We play football now. Some people have even put up some basketball nets. I've started running again. I'd almost forgotten just how many muscles are in the human leg. My arms ache all over from push-ups. Oh, I still hate push-ups, but it makes for a good healthy ache not a bone tired, exhaustion ache.

I tell you though, this place has more gossip floating around than Grandma's Homestudy Club and the old farmers sitting in front of the Barbershop put together! Everybody has a different theory for when we are leaving and what will happen when we get home. The latest rumor says we will get a fourteen-day administrative leave when we get home, but we won't be able to leave the Fort Hood area. Regular leave can be put in for after a recovery period (cleaning up time.) I have also heard that leaves will go in alphabetical order. If that is true, I don't know how we will get our car from you, but these are all rumors, for now.

Well, I better get to answering some Iowa letters! I love and miss you so much, but I feel I can see some light at the end of this tunnel.

Love, Mary E.

March 9, 1991
Dear Mom, Grandma and Grandpa,

I feel safe in writing to Iowa for Grandma and Grandpa. I trust by the time this letter gets home, you two will have not only returned from your visit to California, but have recovered! I hope you had a nice visit with Aunt JoAnn! It's nice to know life goes on.

I received two birthday cards today! Guess from who?? Thanks, Mom! Thanks, Grandma and Grandpa! Grandma, I wish you hadn't spent your bridge club high card prize money on my card. Although, I really loved it. I am sending you a hug in return!

Mom, I wish you would quite worrying about me! Yeah, knock it off or I'll just come over there and...well I'll think of something! I sure love and miss you all heaps and piles!

Love, Mary E.

March 9, 1991
Dear Jason,

Want to hear a good joke? Some reservist cook that just got here in February was trying to tell me that everyone that got here before November has gone home. I told him he should get better sources next time he wants spread a rumor. He looked at me with condescension, and I snapped, "I got here on the 8th of October." His reply, "Oh."

I keep thinking, Tiger Brigade should be moving down around here. If you got to the PX, I might run into you. That would be cool. Do you remember Sergeant S from the orderly room? She is here now. Six weeks to the day after having her first baby, she was on the plane over here. Her husband is over here too. I asked who was taking care of her little girl. She wistfully answered, "My mother." How hard that must be. On the other hand, Sergeant K was whining that she hadn't seen her husband for almost two weeks. I wanted to punch her in the nose. I've stopped listening to the radio, because I'm simply tired of hearing everyone being so happy to be reunited. I'd feel a little better about everyone else's joy if there seemed to be a reunion in sight for us. Oh well, I love you either way.
Love, Mary E.

March 10, 1991
Dear Jason,

I have been told to send this to you incase you get home before me. I suppose you should send one to me too if you can. Hope you get to use it!
Love, Mary E.

I, PFC Mary E. Stabe, give PFC Jason T. Stabe permission to receive our household goods out of storage. Please afford him every and all privileges as though he were me.

March 13, 1991
Dear Jason,

Guess where I am? We have moved back into the desert with old 312th. I walked down to B Company to see if they knew anything about your unit. None of the GSRs are back. I can't wait to see you. I keep thinking you will show up here out of the blue one day. I know it seems unreasonable for you guys on that side of the country move back here only to turn around and go back, but since it's illogical I keep expecting the Army to do it!

It makes me sad to think one man is responsible for so much destruction. Yet just think, we are part of the termination of that very destruction. You should be proud of yourself. I know I am!

We picked up mail before coming here, and I had three letters from you, February 11,14 and 15. You sounded so sad. I sure wish I could make it better for you. I'm sorry that you were passed over for promotion. Makes me wonder who is being promoted? Probably no one, but the saps back in the states who can look the part. Please try not to be sad, we're going home soon. Everyday is one step closer to getting home.

Love, Mary E.

March 14, 1991

Dear Jason,

I got a letter from you today. It was dated January 29th. What a mail system. I keep asking around about you guys. Apparently, Tiger brigade doesn't want to come back, can't imagine why? Words can't describe how much I hate waiting right now. Oh sweetie, I can't wait until we don't have to write anymore. I want to kiss you so much!

Your mom sent me a package that had a music tape from a radio station in Portland. It was really weird to listen to something other than Armed Forces Radio. It was neat to hear a radio station you've grown up with. I can't wait to see your home in Oregon. I had guard at D-rear with a guy from The Dalles. He said I would love Portland and Oregon as well. I think he's right. Well, I can't imagine this can go on much longer so see you soon. I love you!

Love, Mary E.

March 15, 1991

Dear Mom,

Boy, I want to come home! Maybe you could write to President Bush for me! Just kidding, Mom, really, I'm just kidding! I could really go for a pizza, too! I'm sure you could tuck one into an envelope, no problem!

I got a letter from Uncle Jim today. The date on it was December 10, 1990! I couldn't believe it. I sure miss you, but I love you even more!

Love, Mary E.

March 15, 1991
Dear Grandma,

No, I haven't seen Jason yet. I keep a look out for him though. There are so many rumors around, it is hard to know what to believe. I have heard the 2AD wants to go home on it's own, but 1st CAV wont let them. Who knows? Just getting home is the main objective.

I got your card today. I loved the bunny on it! It was so cute! Thanks for sending it to me. Thanks too for the cookies. Sergeant W loves your cookies. I believe she would steal the whole box if I didn't keep my eye on her, ha! I really appreciate all the other things you included as well. Thanks for the film. I will take your advice and take some more pictures. Some of the guys are even harder to photograph than me! They run away or cover their faces whenever I try.

Dad has been writing and asking, "How does it feel not to keep your mask and weapon with you all the time?" I kept thinking, "What's he talking about? We are still dragging them everywhere!" This morning that changed! We were allowed to lock them up. I feel so free! It's nice, but I still keep checking and looking for them all the time.

Well, lunch break is almost over so I better get going. I sure love and miss you, Grandma!
Love, Mary E.

March 15, 1991
Dear Jason,

Thought I'd say hi again. The Colonel just held a formation and praised us for doing so well. He even mentioned some sections by name including Bat-D for a job well done! HA! He also said we probably wouldn't be out of here for forty-five days! When we all groaned, he reminded us it could be sooner. Sometimes, Sweetie, I don't know if I can take these people anymore! Sergeant K with her constant humming, Sergeant W talking to herself that turns into screaming and Sergeant V screaming back at the radio as if it can hear her and that's only when she's not doing that those animal noises, grunts and groans. Naturally, I'm sure I do absolutely nothing to annoy them! Oh, well.
Love, Mary E.

March 16, 1991
Dear Jason,

I finally just gave up and went to sleep. Good way to shut everyone and everything out. Gives me extra time with you since dreams are still all we have. Man, these 6:00am formations to go on to nothing is getting really old

I've got news. I'm not sure if it's good or bad or if it will even make any difference. We had to turn in a priority list for going home. Sergeant T is first and I'm number 2 on Bat-D's list since we're "homeless." Rumor has it that there might be a flight out of here March 24th. Now, if we get slots or not or who knows if Bat-d gets to send people. Just more unanswered questions, more rumors.

I'm still wondering what the deal is about you guys. I hear so many reports, yes, you have to come here because your old unit 522 no longer exists. I hear you're all ready gone or you're going home as 2AD blah, blah, blah. Sure wish I knew something, anything substantial. Knowing my luck, you'll probably come to here the day after I leave or something like that. I can't take too much more of this separation stuff!

Your mom sent me a Doonesbury cartoon about 1st Cav. 2AD makes the paper for heroic efforts and 1st CAV makes the funny papers! She also sent me a Cathy that made me laugh. It was too close to the truth of the first time I tried to cook chicken for you. I called my mom about potatoes and my grandma about the chicken.

I promise you, I'm going to learn how to cook and be a good wife. You deserve the best, and I want to be the best for you, as long as you let me know just what that would be. Oh, I wish we could see each other I'm getting really bad. I'm daydreaming way too much lately. People are always catching me with my mind off into space, and they have a good laugh at me. Laugh if they want, but the only way I get to see you is by my own mental image. Tell you what, I am sick of Memorex. I want the live Jason. Can you tell I am getting a little impatient? Are you laughing? Are you saying, "When were you ever patient?" Knock it off! I'm doing my best, dear.
Love, Mary E.

March 17, 1991
Dear Jason,

Happy St. Patrick's Day. We got the official word your Tiger Brigade is now 1ˢᵗ Cav's 3ʳᵈ Brigade, so we have just become rapid deployment like 82ⁿᵈ and 101ˢᵗ· Well, whooptie, joy! How about El Salvador next Christmas?

Sometimes I wonder if we're ever going to get home or stay home or even be together! I really need a new job. I can't stand this unintelligent intelligence. I know I have a bad attitude that would be greatly helped if I could see you!

Now, I have to tell you about my dream last night. It was kind of freaky. Your parents built a new house in Portland, so my whole family was going to go out there for a house warming. You went out two weeks before me because I was going to drive out with my mom, grandma and grandpa. Boy, did I miss you. That doesn't sound unusual, does it? Anyway, we arrived. Your mom was a nervous wreck waiting for us because she wanted everything perfect for us. The house was a gorgeous, a huge mansion. We were all overwhelmed at the luxury. Your dad had his own cocktail bar room. It had a moveable recipe menu for drinks, only the manufacture screwed up and put a Betty Crocker cookbook in by accident. Your dad said in an embarrassed hush, "I'll have to get that changed." The kitchen was really "retro." It was probably similar to kitchen your parents had when they were first married. It was very 60s psychedelic.

Your parents and I were going up stairs to show my mom and grandparents their rooms. I was on the top of the grand staircase and you came in the double front door with your parents' two cocker spaniels. I guess the cats from reality had been turned into dogs. I ran down the stairs into you arms. We hugged for a long long time. Then you asked me, "How do you like it?" When I looked up at you to answer I saw you had grown a beard! Yes, in two weeks. It looked very distinguished, and I pulled back from you and tugged the bottom of it. I said, "It has to go in the spring." You chuckled at me as you nodded your head. We took off outside, walking arm in arm. It was spring and the lilacs were out. Are there a lot of lilacs in Oregon like there are in Iowa? Anyway, I ran in front of you and picked off a branch and it smelled so good. Just to let you know, I really do love lilacs.

Just as we were ready to go around the corner on our walk, my sister, Susan, came driving up the road like a bat out of hell. She was shouting and screaming about a tornado. She had fled to Oregon because a tornado had devastated Fredericksburg. We took her in the house and everyone gathered around to hear the news. Mom's place was gone. Grandma and Grandpa's was gone. Everything was gone. Susan decided to drive home with Mom, Grandma and Grandpa while I was to stay with you. They were getting ready to leave and you took your wallet to give my grandma some money. I said, "Don't give her that! She'll never take it!" But she looked so sad, dejected. To my shock, she opened her purse for you to drop bills inside it. They were all so distraught to have learned their homes were destroyed.

I was so torn. I wanted to stay with you, but I wanted to help them, too. Sensing my agitation, you pulled me close and kissed me with such tender love. You didn't even have to ask what I was thinking. You knew I was worried for them. Boy was I mad, waking right when I was getting the kisses. I do wonder what it all meant. It was so vivid!

I keep reading in the Bible and the Chaplain even spoke of it today that we need patience. I keep thinking there is a good reason why God hasn't reunited us yet. Somehow we'll be together again. But oh, I miss you so much! It's hard too not getting mail since our last move. I guess it should catch up to me here, someday.

Know what I want for my birthday? Right, You! Preferably on a plane with me going home, but you, you, you! Any shape, any form.
Love, Mary E.

March 21, 1991
Dear Mom,

Well, I'm still here. Big surprise, huh? I think Jason might be coming home before me, but not by much if at all. Sounds pretty conclusive, huh? No one really seems to know anything and even when they think they do, they end up being wrong. So, we wait. I sure am ready to sit in a bathtub with bubbles, eat pizza and watch TV. No, not all at the same time, well, come to think of it, maybe all at the same time!

Saturday is the big 2-4. Is that old or what? I will be two dozen years old. Well, I suppose there isn't much I can do about it, but to let it come. I love you!
Love, Mary E.

March 23, 1991
Dear Mom,

Hmm? Gee, what's so special about today? Let's see. 24 years ago, you went to Bridge Club, came home with a backache, and decided it was time to go to the hospital. I seem to recall you kept getting in trouble with your doctor because you were always off visiting other rooms and drinking coffee and he could never find you. Am I right? Of course I am! Wow, I am 24 years old.

To be honest, it was a pretty miserable day. It was very windy. It rained and poured and rained even more. I always thought it never rained in the desert. I have heard this is an exceptionally wet year due to the oil fires affecting the atmosphere. Naturally, our tent leaks, but I have figured out a way to hang my rain poncho over my cot to keep it dry. We got soaking wet anyway because we had to quickly dig small trenches to divert the water away from the tents. The water just sits on the top of the sand and collects. It doesn't run. It doesn't sink in. It just sits. So, we had to give it the opportunity to run somewhere.

The whole camp was a maze of trenches full of water. I can hear you telling me how much I used to enjoy building rivers and dams and getting wet when I was a kid. Today, I just felt like a dirty wet dog. Probably smelled as bad too! Then after all water finally leeched into the sand, we had to fill all the trenches back in. I must admit, I'm whining. I know, I can't expect to be exempt from annoying details like digging and filling trenches just because it's my birthday.

The day wasn't a total bust either. Aaron and Davy got me a birthday present. I was so shocked when first, they came to my tent, and second, they came bearing a gift. Guys, especially here, aren't known for their sentimental thoughts, but it was greatly appreciated. No, I didn't get sappy on them and cry or hug them or anything. I just really appreciated the thought, thanked them heartily, and shared some more of my cookies. The present was a brass tray with three small-stemmed brass cups to match. I don't know if it has any cultural significance, but it is pretty.

The best part of the whole day was news or I guess a rumor. Word is Jason's unit will be meeting us at the port! Oh, I can't wait to see him! It would be really great if we would get to go home together. Home, now that's something to hope for. If I had a cake with candles, that is what I would wish for!

I know this wasn't the best birthday I've ever had, and it might even be the worst, but it is definitely one for the record books! I miss you so much, Mom, and love you even more.
Love, Mary E.

March 31, 1991
Dear Mom,
Hey, take a look at this!

Hi! Mom, Yes this is Jason! Finally Mary and I are together again. Hopefully we will be home soon. I hope everything is going well.

Love, Jason

Happy Easter! What a wonderful Easter it is, too with Jason here! We are having a nice Easter. We're out here in the middle of the desert kind of half picnicking, half sunbathing, and basically just taking it easy. It feels strange to actually do something pleasant for once, except the flies are horrible!

As of today, our date for coming home (to Texas anyway) is April 21st. That will be one day late of our first anniversary, but now that Jason is here at this site, that's ok. It's just so nice to get to see him on a more regular basis.

Well, believe it or not, I got promoted. They are supposed to pin it on me tomorrow, April Fool's Day. I sure hope it's not a fool! I'm so excited Jason will be here to see it. I didn't think it was a big deal, but I am getting pretty excited. So, after tomorrow I will be Specialist Mary E. Pretty cool, huh?

Mom, I have to tell you something funny! Jason's mom sent me a tape she made of Jason's favorite radio station complete with the commercials and all. Anyway, the DJ said it was 3:35pm and I looked down at my watch and it really was 3:35pm. Isn't that weird?
Love, Mary E.

April 16, 1991
Dear Family,
I'm sorry I haven't been writing. We have been so busy getting ready to come home! We finally convoyed to the port at Dhahran. It was long and nasty convoy for me. 201 has sprung a nasty exhaust leak right at the manifold and all the exhaust just keeps pouring into the cab. Aaron and I drove a good part of the way with our front windshield out, but it is hard on the eyes to have the wind

whipping at them constantly. The fumes weren't so bad when we were driving on the hard ball, but when we had to go slow it was almost unbearable.

I have taken several pictures of camels, sand dunes, an oasis, and oil well fires for you, all out the window of my truck. For the most part though, it was a pretty quiet trip to the coast, but long. I think it took about fifteen hours.

Once we got here, we were assigned to Kobar Towers. These were real buildings with real toilets and real bathtubs! The story has it that these were built to house Bedouins, but they didn't have any desire to live in them, so we get to use them. I had to flush the toilet just to make sure I wasn't seeing things. I have found I can't take a hot bath, tepid water is all I can use right now. I suppose after all cold showers it's too much of a shock to my system. We've mostly been doing laundry in the tubs. Our room has drying clothes hanging in all available spots.

I am sharing a room with six other women. I am not with my Bat-D sergeants because they are all NCOs who only have four to a room. I don't care how many people I share with, it's pretty nice to have walls that don't move or have poles and a bathroom I don't have to put boots on to walk to. Jason is one floor above me.

Our first job when we got here was to clean our weapons and turn them in. I still find myself looking for it at times. Then, we started cleaning the vehicles and equipment to get them ready to be shipped home. We scrubbed and washed and cleaned for days. Each and every decoy had to be clean and sand free. After each item was finished, it had to be inspected and officially sealed. I guess the authorities didn't want us to confiscate any materials. Talk about a daunting task, but we finally finished late last night after eight days. During the day while we all sat down to take a quick break, a soldier came up to me and said, "You know, we've been watching you, and we think you're the strongest woman we've ever seen!" I didn't even have time to respond before he and his unit were back to work on their own equipment. I'm pretty sure that was a compliment, I hope so anyway. Our vehicles have been turned over to the people loading the ships and I'm not sure if I will miss 201 or not. Well, it isn't as if I won't ever see it again.

Now we have a free day before we clean the barracks and get assigned a flight. We aren't allowed to go anywhere except for this open air market square about a block away. They have trinkets to buy, and camel rides. A place to buy shirts and another selling pants. A place under a tent to buy ice cream and another to buy chicken and another with fruit. There is also a mail drop point. You can send boxes, but you have to pay for them, no MPS free. Jason and I have decided to ship home as much as we can. It will save us from having a lot to haul around when we first get back. We have to keep issue items with us, but things like my birthday present and books can be sent ahead. I wish there was a phone center to call and let you know we are so close to coming home.

Jason and I walk around together or sit out front talking. Neither of us is allowed on the other's floor and it is practically killing me not to be able to kiss him or even hold his hand. I know we are practically home free, but it's pretty hard. Almost like dangling that unreachable carrot in front of the horse! Can't be long now! I love and miss you all so much, but the light at the end of this war tunnel is growing brighter by the second!
Love, Mary E.

April 20, 1991
Hi Everybody!

I'm here! I'm back in the USA! I can hardly believe it myself! Jason and I arrived back at Fort Hood last night (or I should say this morning.) It was our first anniversary. After giving up birthdays and holidays, the one occasion I didn't want to give up was our first anniversary, and we made it! Thanks to someone trying to smuggle contraband home, it bumped a whole company, and we got to slide right into their slot. Not a soul complained about leaving a day early! I don't think the other company was feeling so generous to their culprit!

Until we actually took off, I had this fear they would call us back and tell us we still had to stay. It was nice to be in the air and start putting miles in between Saudi Arabia and me! We had a four-hour layover in Frankfurt, Germany, so they let us off the plane. The first thing I noticed was the smell of the trees. I couldn't believe how wonderful it was to smell trees and see green. It was neat to see Germany. Granted it was all a bird's eye view, but I have seen Frankfurt.

We were flying on a Delta airlines plane, and they served us a steak dinner. We were making jokes about airline food, but I tell you that steak was the best thing I had tasted in a good long while. I thought we should try and get some sleep, but we were all so excited and joyous about going home that none of us could squelch the adrenalin.

It was 3:00am when we landed in Texas. I really didn't expect anyone to greet us, but much to my surprise, there was the 1st CAV band playing for our descent down the steps and onto blessed American soil. It was so great! Even more to our surprise were the people lining the airfield fence, cheering for us. Finally, we got to see all of the support we had been hearing about, and it was incredibly heartwarming and extraordinarily gratifying. We had to wait for a debriefing, which pretty much consisted of waiting, which as you know is so unusual for the Army. There was a short welcome home speech and instructions about when and where to be next. We loaded onto buses that drove us from the airfield back to Fort Hood. As the bus drove through the front gate, a group of AmVets were saluting us. I was impressed and so proud. There in the middle of the night stood men, who to me were the real heroes of America. They were standing at attention-honoring me! WOW! To be honest, I cried. Seeing those men and the sheer joy of seeing familiar sights and smells, I just sobbed with relief. I'll tell you, I wasn't alone.

When we pulled up to the gym to unload, there were hundreds of people cheering. We had to make a formation to be officially dismissed, but the families were cheering so loud we couldn't hear the commander say, "COMPANY, DISMISSED!" We didn't even know we were released until he turned around and walked off. Families came flooding off the bleachers and poured over the floor like a tidal wave. Jason and I had trouble finding one another through the throngs of cheering, euphoric people that were hugging and kissing, crying and laughing all at the same time. When we finally latched on to one another, we grabbed our bags as fast as we could and got outside. Where did we go from there? We didn't have a home to go to, yet. Our commander had said we were welcome to stay in the barracks, but would you stay in the barracks with a bunch of other people on your first anniversary? Not to mention the first time in months that you could be absolutely positively alone with your very own husband! So, I am writing this from the lap of flushing toilet, hot shower, sand free luxury of the Hilton Hotel. Let me tell you, it is nice to be home!
Love, Mary E.

May 1, 1990

Dear Dairy Day Board,

    I am thrilled and delighted by your request for Jason and me to act as Grand Marshals of the Dairy Day Parade. We would be pleased to be honored guests of Dairy Day. I can think of nothing more appealing than being in my hometown in June. I have so missed the green grass, the lowing of cattle and the moist fragrant breeze of early summer. I will also appreciate the opportunity to thank in person all the wonderful folks that supported us by their letters, cards and packages. I feel truly blessed to be a member of such a caring community and glorious country. Thank you so much for this privilege and for the privilege to represent our community in service to our nation.

Most Respectfully,

Specialist Mary E. McFarland-Stabe, United States Army